Advertising Collectibles

of Times Past

By Dorothy Hammond

with Robert Hammond

To our children
Kurby, Kristy, and Kiper

Published and Manufactured
in the
United States of America
by the

WALLACE-HOMESTEAD BOOK COMPANY

Des Moines, Iowa 50305

Library of Congress
Catalog Card Number 74-75950

Contents

Acknowledgements

The authors wish to express their gratitude to the many individuals and institutions mentioned below, who have supplied historical information, provided pictorial material, and given generously of their time to make this volume possible.

John Mebane, The Antiques Journal
Ward Kimball, Walt Disney Productions
Henry Griffin
Mrs. Leon Rebarber
James B. Beam Distilling Company
Watkins Products, Inc.
Mr. and Mrs. Hugh W. Parker, British Hollow Antiques
R. T. Shufflebotham, Libby, McNeill and Libby
Harry E. Ellis, Dr. Pepper Company
James E. Dicks, Clark Gum Company
Mr. and Mrs. Nelson H. Poe
Miss Boyd Bowers, H. J. Heinz Company
Thomas T. Gray, Brown-Forman Distillers Corporation
Fred T. Bussee, National Distillers Products Company
T. J. LoCascio, Planters
Elinor Block, Standard Brands Incorporated
Helen B. Bundick, Can Manufacturers Institute, Inc.
Pauline J. Grieger, Johnson Wax
Mr. and Mrs. Jack Muzio
Ray McGuffin
Lucille Nitzburg, The Quaker Oats Company
Wilbur G. Kurtz, Jr., The Coca-Cola Company
Pat Wagner, Western Publications, Inc.
George O. Bird, Henry Ford Museum, Greenfield Village
Mrs. Don Johnson
Laurence W. McKee, The Prudential Insurance Company
Don Reschenberg, Joseph Schlitz Brewing Company
D. V. Brondyke, Ferry Morse Seed Company
Robert C. Hare, Carnation Company
Willar Kayser, Hulman and Company
Grace Ellis, Pabst Brewing Company
Mary Hoban, National Biscuit Company
E. M. Maguire, Thomas J. Lipton, Inc.
Thomas J. Carroll, Anheuser-Busch, Inc.
T. L. Paulsen, The Folger Coffee Company
Franklin Halverson
Joe D. Thomas, Kellogg Company
Mrs. John H. Gale
Doran P. Welch, General Foods Corporation
E. W. Spear, Armour and Company
M. W. Eichers, Brown and Bigelow
Jay A. Clark, Campbell Soup Company
Muriel R. O'Callaghan, Distilled Spirits Institute, Inc.
Miller Brewing Company
J. V. Kern, U.S. Borax and Chemical Corporation
H. H. Winter, Glidden-Durkee

Mrs. Kay Archer
Ken Bassett
Pauline Hill
Morgan Guenther, United States Brewers Association, Inc.
Henry W. Bahrenburg, American Brands, Inc.
William W. Wallace, Falstaff Brewing Corporation
Huntley and Palmers, Reading, England
Sylvia Schaberl, AB (America) Ltd
Mr. and Mrs. Lee O. Martin
Mrs. Lillian Hammond
Mr. and Mrs. Edwin Turpin
Mrs. Wanda Sanders
Mr. and Mrs. Henry Vanis
Mrs. Patricia Schoonmaker, Doll Research Projects
General Mills
Swift and Company
R. J. Reynolds Tobacco Company
Mr. and Mrs. Charles Freeman
Craig Vanis
Mr. and Mrs. Harold Manning
Sue Snyder
Mrs. Neta Crowe
Mr. and Mrs. Paul Harmon
Hershey Foods Corporation
Mr. and Mrs. Wesley Garton
Mr. and Mrs. LaVerne Reinert
Barton K. Battaile

SMALL CHANGE TRAY
CIRCA 1890

BIBLIOGRAPHY

CAIN, William — *Out of the Cracker Barrel*
CLYMER, Floyd — *Early Advertising*
HEIMANN, Robert K. — *Tobacco & Americans*
COCHRAN, Thomas C. — *The Pabst Brewing Company*
MARTIN, Milward W. — *Twelve Full Ounces*
GRAY, James — *Business Without Boundary*
ANDERSON, Sonja & Will — *Beers, Breweries & Breweriana*
COLEMAN, Dorothy S., Elizabeth A. and Evelyn J. — *The Collector's Encyclopedia of Dolls*
PETTIT, Ernest L. — *The Book of Collectible Tin Containers*
DAVIS, Marvin & Helen — *Tobacco Tins*
DIETZ, Lawrence — *Soda-pop Art* (February 9, 1969, issue of WEST Magazine, a weekly publication of The Los Angeles Times)
NEWHALL, Ruth Waldo — *The Folger Way*
BRAHAM, Michael — *History That Goes Hand in Hand with Reading*

TIN MATCH HOLDER
Tin holder, 3½" high, features a small boy cutting bread. Barrel attached to the front holds matches. Ceresota Flour Company.

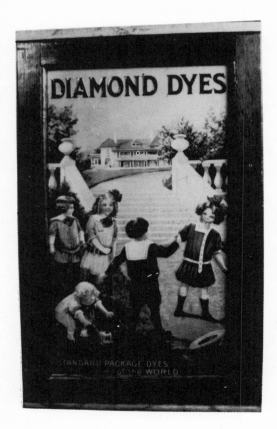

WOOD CABINET WITH TIN
PAINTED FRONT

These decorative fire buckets of another era are quite elusive today.

Introduction

The word advertising comes from the French word *avertir* meaning to notify. Advertising is actually as old as trade, probably beginning with what present day businessmen call personal selling, or word of mouth advertising. In essence, it informs people of the various advantages of a product, an idea, or a service. Advertising has many media — newspapers, magazines, television, radio, billboards, window displays, direct mail, novelties, etc., each designed to make the public aware of a product or service and encourage them to buy it.

The earliest form of advertising was probably outdoor advertising, dating back to messages carved

on large stone pillars and tablets in ancient Egypt. These "ads" were placed near the main roads, just as present-day billboards are. In Babylon 5,000 years ago, merchants used symbols as advertisements. The Sign of the Bush over a doorway advertised a wine shop; whereas today, modern electric signs flash their spectacular messages in colored lights. And in ancient Greece, town criers shouted advertising messages in the streets. Today, radio and television permeate the sound waves with friendly and frequent persuasion.

The invention of movable type about 1440 made it possible to distribute advertising messages more widely than ever before. William Caxton introduced printing to England in the year 1480 and prepared the first known advertisement, a handbill. His ad announced the sale of a book and was posted on church doors. The first newspaper ad appeared in Germany in 1525, advertising a medicine for sale. And during the 1600s printed handbills, posters, and newspaper advertising became common.

When manufacturing developed, few persons could read, as universal free education did not exist until the 1800s. Therefore businessmen used symbols. For example, a shoemaker used a sign shaped like a shoe over his shop door, or a jeweler displayed a dummy clock. Later when words were added, the symbols became trade signs.

Advertising and industry grew up together in the United States. The first newspaper advertising appeared in the Boston News-Letter founded in 1704. From about 1750 until 1850, more and more newspapers appeared in the United States, and fees from advertising became their principal means of revenue. During the 1880s, John E. Powers — frequently referred to as the father of modern advertising — pioneered a new kind of advertising copy. His short, simple words sounded honest and sincere — thus his methods influence all advertising today.

The first successful American magazine, The Journal Magazine founded by Benjamin Franklin in 1743, carried paid advertising. And during the early

Cutting Ice on the Mississippi
1860-1880

LANGENECKERT.

A CENTURY OF BREWING IN ST. LOUIS
©1964, Falstaff Brewing Corporation, St. Louis, Mo

COURTESY FALSTAFF INTERNATIONAL MUSEUM OF BREWING

1900s, Cyrus H. K. Curtis, founded the first big national magazines that became powerful advertising media. Radio advertising began in 1922, and television advertising in 1939.

Today, with new collectors appearing on the scene daily, the serious collecting of early advertising mementos is becoming more widespread. Enthusiasts soon discover that searching out advertising memorabilia is actually an endless adventure. Literally hundreds of individual fields within this broad scope offer a multitude of choices. Values are going up — a sad note, perhaps, but also a good one because it forces the collector to be more discriminating and build a more meaningful collection. Once you are into this collecting field, really into it, expect your tastes to change — and all for the better.

Nostalgia has created the current craze to acquire early advertising memorabilia, because in our hectic, parlous, plastic world today, the older generation as well as the young seem to need to return to this kind of thing.

This book was planned as a pictorial guide to advertising collectibles. Most of the objects shown are not beyond possible acquisition by the reader. However, it is true that in several instances, illustrations are of specimens in museums or collections of manufacturers. In such instances, identical or similar articles are known to exist — either in antique shops or in private collections.

It is the hope of the authors that this book will enrich the lives of all those interested in collecting early advertising mementos that revise the craftsmanship of previous generations. These have a staying quality and will always be possessions of value, no matter how the vagaries of popularity may shift.

Advertising Calendars

the history of calendars

Calendars, particularly the fancy novelty type made by Raphel Tuck & Son, London, and others are included in the field of advertising collectibles. Some firms published unusual ones showing outstanding designs. It will be of interest that post card calendars were also produced during the last century.

It was in 1752 that the English speaking world finally decided to get in step with nearly everyone else by adopting the Gregorian system of keeping track of days, months and years.

Due to errors in computing time, however, the Julian calendar used up to that time by England and her colonies was eleven days behind the Gregorian calendar named after Pope Gregory XIII. To catch up in a hurry, eleven days had to be wiped out or "annihilated" as the people of the time put it.

Thus, it was ordered that the calendar for 1752 should skip from September 2 to September 14. This caused considerable confusion.

Tenants and landlords squabbled about rents; businessmen in general were upset about contract performance, delivery of goods, payments of bills and other fiscal operations hinging on the calendar. Anniversaries, birthdays, weddings all were knocked askew by the sudden loss of time.

To put the finger on the cause of all this grief, you have to dig back into history and take a look at man's first puny attempts to count days, months and years.

Since the first cave man whacked at a handy tree with his stone axe to mark passage of one day, man has tried many ways to keep track of time accurately.

Astronomy is the basis of all calendars. When the earth turns on its axis we have the day. The revolution of the earth around the sun makes the year. The passage of the moon around the earth produces the month.

To keep track of these goings-on sounds kind of simple. However, to measure these journeys in the matter of minutes, even seconds, is a job for crack astronomers and scientists.

Spring, we say, begins on the 21st of March. But this is just a rough approximation. Just what second during that day, or the day before or after, does the vernal equinox visit us each year?

A few minutes or hours doesn't sound like much in computing a year but even a minor error can add up over the years — and centuries.

As early as 3500 BC the Sumerians came up with a calendar. It was workable even if the year was only 354 days, 11 days short of a true solar year.

Along came the Babylonians. They drove a stake into the ground to mark the shift of the rising sun to record seasonal change. This calculation of time by seasons was all right for their uncomplicated life, but these early timekeepers were as far off as before. They had to make adjustment for 11 days each year.

This was easy. They merely shoved in an extra month every now and then to bring the calendar up to par. This was rough on the farmer and businessman but the tax gatherer must have gloated over the chance for extra levies.

The Chaldeans narrowed down the margin of error in about 500 BC to a mere half hour a year. The Egyptians who had fixed a year back in 4236 BC, had been toying with a calendar ever since.

They proved even sharper than the Chaldeans and brought the error down to only 11 minutes and 14 seconds each year.

Along came the Romans and in 46 BC Julius Caesar instituted more calendar reform. He kept the same Egyptian error and to catch up on lost time, he ordered that 46 BC be given an added 90 days. This became the "Year of Confusion" in history and it is easy to imagine the consternation caused by the drastic alteration of time.

All this time, astronomers worked constantly to try to reconcile the calendar with the heavenly movements. Meanwhile this 11 minute and 14 second shortage each year began to accumulate. By the 16th century, the year was 10 days out of kilter.

The farmers who sowed, tilled and reaped according to the feasts of the Church, were left in a whirl. The moon, sun and stars seemed to be off the beam and the seasons all out of whack. The poor

COURTESY PRUDENTIAL INSURANCE COMPANY

farmer found his small world was topsy-turvy. He was shocked to find that religion and agriculture just didn't hit it off together any more.

Meantime, Pope Gregory XIII began looking into the problem. Setting aside a room in the Vatican (still known as the Calendar Room) he put his best scientists to work. Here they toiled until they produced a calendar which, with an extra day every four years to take up the slack, worked out pretty well.

The margin of error in this computation, though small, will account for the loss of only one day in more than 3,000 years.

The Gregorian calendar was adopted by Catholic countries in 1565. Protestant England and her American colonies still stuck by their Julian calendar.

So we come to the 18th century with the two calendars functioning almost side by side, one 11 days behind the other.

Finally the English parliament decided enough was enough. It voted to get back in step with other countries. To adjust things rapidly, the September 1752 jump was ordered and for once England and America were even with most of the rest of the world.

It was a busy English speaking world occupied with trade and territorial squabbling which had to absorb the dramatic calendar revision of 1752.

In America, the anxieties of early colonial life were disappearing. The powdered wig and hoop skirt, the knee breeches and whale-bone stays marked the indulgence in taste for fine raiment which followed the pattern in England.

Benjamin Franklin, who is generally credited with introducing the calendar as we know it today into America, in his thorough and painstaking way did not let this change pass unnoticed.

He devoted most of his 1752 edition of Poor Richard's Almanac to the calendar. He traced its origin and development, the various ways of computing time and the reason for the sudden switch to a new kind of time-telling device. His readers were well aware that there was more to making a calendar than merely printing names and numbers on a sheet. After the demise of Franklin's almanac in 1757, others sprang up to furnish the early American businessmen and homes with calendars. These ventures continued on until the late 1880s, and some are still being published.

Early in the century almanacs carried advertising, or at least the name of the publisher. In 1836 one published in New York carried an ad for pills and others soon after put in a plug for vegetable powders and syrups.

HARTFORD INSURANCE COMPANY

On June 27, 1890, in a little village on the Connecticut River a meeting of great importance in the progress of America took place. Held in Hartford at Ransom's Inn, it was the first stockholders' meeting of the Hartford Fire Insurance Company. Chartered a month earlier by the Connecticut General Assembly with a working capital of $15,000, it was the first insurance company to be incorporated in the state. From this beginning, through test and triumph, the Hartford progressed to fame.

One of the most familiar trademarks in the world is that of the Hartford Stag. Early drawings showed a stag (sometimes called a hart) fording a stream — therefore, hart/ford. In 1851 a famous English artist, Sir Edwin Landseer, painted the majestic stag, "Monarch of the Glen," and an adaptation of this stag later became the emblem which symbolizes to millions of people the strength and protection of the company.

THE PRUDENTIAL STORY

Down through the ages the Rock of Gibraltar has excited man's interest and awe. Today, it is the world's best-known symbol of financial security.

This symbol had its beginning in 1895, twenty years after the founding of The Prudential Insurance Company of America.

That was when John F. Dryden, Prudential's founder, began to search for a symbol that would depict the financial strength and stability of his highly successful company. He had brought Prudential up from a shaky financial start to a position of strength, with almost $15 million in assets and a unique reputation for paying claims promptly.

One advertising agency, engaged to find a suitable device, spent several months in fruitless effort. In early 1896 another agency took on the challenge of creating the ideal design. Mortimer Remington presented the idea of the upthrusting rock formation to Dryden, who welcomed it enthusiastically. He felt that everyone would regard this magnificent natural fortress as the epitome of strength and security, and then associate those qualities with Prudential.

Curiously enough, one of the trademark versions of the Rock is an artist's conception rather than an actual scene. The story goes that the artist, after studying several pictures, prepared a composite view in which the land at the base of the 1,400-foot rock face was replaced by lapping waves. Mortimer Remington had protested. As it turned out, Mr. Dryden liked the sketch, and to this day the artist's version still prevails.

Dryden was so interested and enthusiastic that he personally directed the massive advertising campaign the company began in August 1896.

13

COURTESY PRUDENTIAL INSURANCE COMPANY

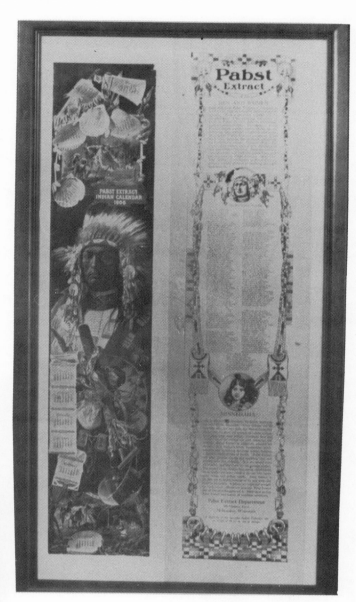

COURTESY PABST BREWING COMPANY

SMALL VINTAGE CALENDAR

PABST MALT EXTRACT CALENDAR — 1907

Originally printed on two sides. Reverse side was photostated and mounted alongside the front in this photograph. Similar calendars were issued annually by Pabst for Best Tonic from 1907 to 1912.

BROWN & BIGELOW

The birth of a calendar as a true advertising medium for businessmen other than those in the printing or allied fields sprang from the necessity of a couple of broke but resourceful newspaper publishers.

Edmond B. Osborne and Thomas D. Murphy were college chums in the 1880s. Partners after graduation in operating a weekly paper at Red Oak, Iowa, the young men wanted to run a picture in their publication of a projected new courthouse. Unable to pay for a wood cut since this would use up the entire week's revenue from their paper, Osborne hit on an idea. He outlined to his partner a plan for printing a wall calendar and surrounding it with advertising of local merchants. About 25 businessmen went for the idea and the young advertising calendar pioneers netted $300 on the deal. They put out 1,000 calendars.

Sensing the future in this field, Murphy and Osborne went on to establish their own companies in Red Oak and Clifton, N.J., before the team split to establish their separate firms.

The man who was to found the largest calendar firm in the world today was their first salesman. He was Herbert Huse Bigelow, who teamed up with a printer in 1896 to start Brown & Bigelow in St. Paul, the world's largest advertising specialty company.

In 1903 the first full-color calendar reproductions were offered customers in a subject called "Luscious Fruit." In 1904 the firm followed with the famous girl subject "Cosette," which proved a fast selling item for many years and gave an early forecast of the value of a pretty girl on any type of advertising.

Introduced in these early years were items such as horse covers, cloth caps, pancake turners, fly swatters, watch fobs and similar popular merchandise.

While the company has grown tremendously and ventured into all types of advertising novelties, Brown & Bigelow still remains the foremost calendar maker in the world, turning out 50 million calendars a year.

While most of us are familiar with the conventional calendar block containing the months, it was only after 1900 that this type came into use.

Since then, calendars have branched out into all types and are made of various materials. Metal and plastic calendars in addition to paper products are turned out by the hundreds of thousands by Brown & Bigelow. Calendars are fashioned for home and even for various rooms in the home. They are made for office, for desk, for wall and for personal use.

For the housewife, Brown & Bigelow has developed the pocket calendar. Here in handy little pouches can be kept recipes, grocery slips and other household records. For the farmer, too, the pocket calendar comes in handy as a convenient place to file away his stock and crop records and other farm information.

Colored photograph calendars feature all types of subjects. There are pictures for the mother, for outdoor enthusiast, the lover of flowers, dogs, children. In addition Brown & Bigelow turns out thousands of tailormade jobs for many of America's largest industries.

From a one-room operation in 1896 with one of the partners, Bigelow, its lone salesman, the Brown & Bigelow company has grown to a huge operation with vast plants in St. Paul and Minneapolis.

Certain calendar types and subjects are reserved for specific businessmen under a franchise so that year after year firm and product are identified with the calendar.

The Boy Scout Calendar published exclusively by Brown & Bigelow for 37 years is one of the best in the line. Illustrated by Norman Rockwell, this calendar is specifically designed for public places. The national organization of the Scouts receives royalties on each one of these calendars sold by Brown & Bigelow. This official Boy Scout Calendar is given under franchise to a merchant who may have exclusive right to its use in a specific territory.

The 4-H Club Calendar is published under similar arrangement with royalties going to support the national 4-H camp.

Although early American calendars were designed specifically for hanging in offices and public places, the trend toward home calendars has given impetus to the development of the calendar business.

CALENDARS COURTESY BROWN & BIGELOW

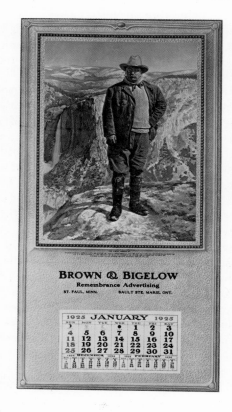

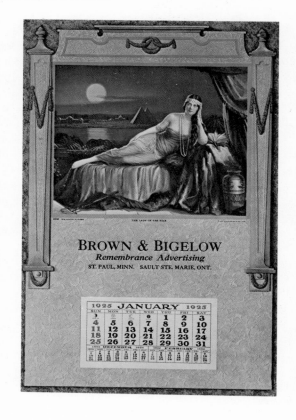

17

Buddy Lee Doll (plastic). Railway Engineer.

Aunt Jemima rag doll, Circa 1910, 13" tall.

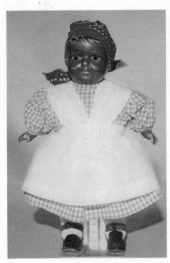

Aunt Jemima Doll (composition body).

Advertising Dolls

Dolls have been used since the last century to promote a product or a company. Some were given away as premiums, while others were sold to the public, or sold to dealers for window and interior store display. Among these was the Buddy Lee doll which was used to promote overalls for the H. D. Lee Mercantile Company. The uniqueness of this doll — size 13", molded hair, painted eyes glancing to the side, and jointed shoulders — and the plan of distribution and use instantly caught on. Since Buddy Lee made his initial appearance in the 1920s, he has appeared in hundreds of windows and stores, and has found his way into thousands of homes. When the doll had served its purpose, it was usually offered for resale by the store's owner.

Undoubtedly among the leaders among rag dolls of longest commercial output, the Aunt Jemima dolls have been intermittently on the market from 1890 until 1942.

Chris Rutt sought for his self-rising pancake flour a character that could be identified with southern cooking. One evening in the autumn of 1889, he attended the local vaudeville, which featured a pair of black-face comedians known as Baker and Farrell. The show-stopper of this particular act was a jazzy, rhythmic New Orleans style cakewalk to a tune called "Aunt Jemima," which Baker performed in the apron and red-bandanna headband of the traditional southern cook.

Here, at last, was the image Rutt sought! He not only used the song's title for the name of his pancake flour, but also the likeness of the southern "mammy" emblazoned on the lithograph posters advertising the Baker and Farrell act. The name Aunt Jemima was placed on a one-pound paper sack as a trademark, along with a wide-eyed, grinning caricature of Aunt Jemima, in what could be described as living color. Now, Rutt was in business.

Unfortunately, merchandising was not within Rutt's means or those of his silent partner who was an expert miller but no promoter. So the Pearl

Milling Company soon ran out of capital and expired. However, the partners retained their valuable asset in the failure, and a few months later with the aid of a new moneyman they organized the Aunt Jemima Manufacturing Company, which was later purchased by the R. T. Davis Milling Company. Davis knew what to do with his acquisition, as he was a master of publicity. He envisioned a living Aunt Jemima to advertise his product. He sent requests to his food-broker friends to be on the lookout for a Negro woman who could demonstrate the self-rising pancake mix at fairs, expositions, and festivals. Here, a new advertising concept was born, which brought a trademark to life. Since that moment of Davis' inspiration, scores of advertisers have introduced living impersonations of their trademarks.

Davis followed other cereal manufacturers by offering boxtop premiums, one of which became the most famous in merchandising history. For one trademark off the carton and twenty-five cents, which paid all the costs, customers received an Aunt Jemima rag doll. The rag doll evolved from an earlier stunt of 1895, when Aunt Jemima pancake flour began to be distributed in cartons, rather than in one-pound sacks. To popularize the new container, Davis printed on it a cutout paper doll of Aunt Jemima, and the promotion was a success.

A decade later, when the company was rising from one of its bankruptcies, the Aunt Jemima rag doll emerged, renewing itself year after year, until a family of rag dolls had been created which included Uncle Mose, and twin moppets Diana and Wade. The dolls enjoyed such great popularity that other concerns became doll conscious, and began to manufacture cloth cut-outs.

Later promotions distributed four million sets of Aunt Jemima-Uncle Mose salt and pepper shakers in polystyrene, and 200,000 dolls in vinyl plastic. And a cookie-jar premium shaped like Aunt Jemima sold 150,000.

On January 15, 1926, the Aunt Jemima Mill was sold to The Quaker Oats Company and Quaker's wholesale distributors put Aunt Jemima into retail stores all over the country for the first time.

The Babbitt at Your Service Cleanser Boy (1916) doll was made by the Modern Toy Company and represented the trademark of the B. T. Babbitt Company. The doll holds a can of cleanser, and is 15 inches tall.

In 1917, the Baby Bunting doll made its appearance, holding a can of Colgate talcum powder.

The Northwestern Consolidated Milling Company began using the trademark Ceresota in 1891, and their mark has been found on rag dolls representing a farmer boy with high boots and hat. Their

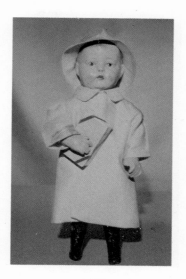

"Uneeda Kid" doll. Red label on sleeve reads: "Trade 'Uneeda Kid' Mark, Patented December 8, 1914," Manufactured by Ideal Novelty & Toy Co., Brooklyn, N.Y.

Campbell Kid Doll (Original Horsman type).

Betsy McCall doll, made by the Ideal Toy Corporation. Copyright date, 1951, McCall Corporation.

"Rastus" doll, advertises Cream of Wheat.

cut-out type rag doll was a form of advertisement for the company, and was probably made from a flour sack. The date of the doll and how long it was distributed is unknown.

The Cinderella doll (circa 1910) was a Naphtha Soap Powder coupon doll. It was dressed in satin, and came with a bisque head and sewed curly wig. This doll came in three sizes — 19, 21, and 26 inches.

Cracker Jack Boy (1917) was produced by the Ideal Novelty and Toy Company. This boy doll was dressed in blue and white sailor suit with cap, and carried a tiny replica of a Cracker Jack box under his arm. The doll represented Rueckheim Bros. & Eckstein.

Dolly Drake (1917) was made by Reliance Novelty Company, with permission of Drake Brothers Company. The doll represented their advertisement of a girl with a cake. It is an unbreakable character doll, dressed in the Kate Greenaway manner with pantalets, a yellow dress with drakes printed on it, and a big yellow baker's hat.

Fairy (1911-1915) was designed by Helen Trowbridge and copyrighted by Horsman. This doll represented the fairy figure in the advertisements for Little Fairy Soap, made by the N. K. Fairbanks Company.

The Happiness dolls were a 1925 line of dolls produced by Louis Wolf & Company, by special arrangement with Happiness Candy Stores. The line included Toddling Toodles (walking doll) and Baby Sunshine.

Puffy is the Quaker Puffed Rice and Puffed Wheat doll. It was printed on cloth (bright blue trousers and cap, with red jacket) and put out in 1930.

The Rastus Chef rag doll dates from the 1930s. It is printed on cloth in colors and is about 19 inches tall without the chef's hat. Rastus was reproduced through the courtesy of the Cream of Wheat Corporation.

Skookum, The Bully Kiddo (1916), was copyrighted by Louis Amberg & Son, who made the doll under exclusive license from the Northwest Fruit Exchange, national advertisers of Skookum apples. The dolls resembled their Indianhead trademark.

Span (1911-1912) is a Dutch girl doll with composition head, round chubby face, hair parted in middle, large eyes, cork-stuffed pink sateen body, and dressed in a striped gingham frock with green suspenders. She wears Dutch shoes. Her mate is Spic, a Dutch boy with big blue eyes, looking downward. He is dressed in red trousers and Dutch shoes. These dolls represented the figures in the advertisements of a metal polish.

"The Selling Fool" Advertising Doll. Made of wood and wood pulp, it has a radio tube head and stands 15½" tall. Made for R.C.A., it was copyrighted by J. L. Kallus in 1926. Maxfield Parrish created the original character. Label on bottom of one foot reads "Art Quality Mfg., Cameo Doll Co., N.Y."

Campbell Kid Doll, cloth torso, 13½" tall. Label on neck reads "Campbell Kid."

COURTESY SARA BARRETT

Hot Point Advertising Doll. Copyrighted by J. L. Kallus. Stove is marked: "Metal Ware Corp., Two Rivers, Wisc., 175 watts, 110 volts, U.S.A."

Vanta baby doll, advertised Vanta baby care products. Vinyl head, rubber body, 21½" tall.

COURTESY SARA BARRETT

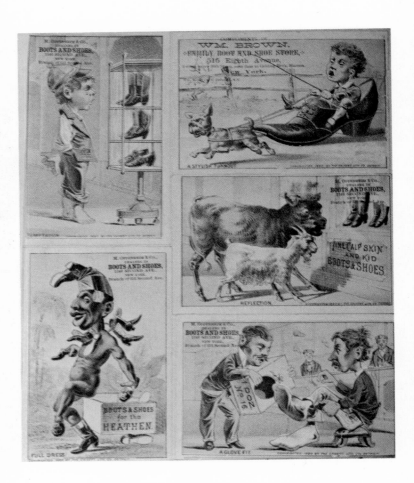

HARRIET REBARBER COLLECTION

Advertising Cards

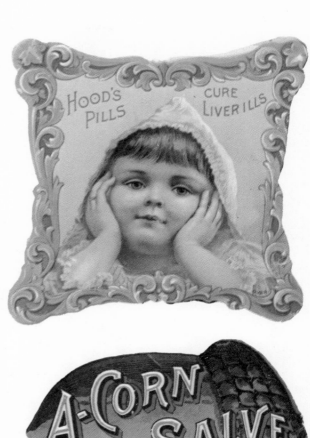

One of the most fascinating fields of collecting today is that of advertising or trading cards. These small pieces of paper Americana are actually works of art, especially designed to capture the attention of the public. They appeal to both young and old, and make an excellent specialty for the collector who has a limited amount of space available for display.

Advertising cards are of various sizes. Some are as small as a calling card, while others are quite large, and most are very colorful. Many were produced by famous lithographers of the day, and sometimes bear their imprints, including that of Currier & Ives. Cards of the 1810-1850 period are now in various older museums and libraries in the East. Unfortunately, few cards are dated, and in many instances, even the most intensive research will fail to disclose the time of use.

Early cards can usually be recognized by the type faces, and the absence of brand names. This group usually advertised a business, rather than a specific product — such as tailor, gunsmith, and dozens of similar occupations. Some of the earlier examples are embossed in color and many are on a high glazed card that was popular for a period. However, the very earliest may be on heavy paper or very light card, without color, glazing, or embossing.

The value of an advertising card depends on the apparent age, subject, size and general attractiveness. And should a well known artist's signature appear on a card, this adds greatly to its value, as does historical significance and quality of printing.

During the 1870s, the early advertising type of card was gradually replaced by colored cards made especially for individual firms. Business men knew that the cards, especially those bearing illustrations in color, were going into collections, thus providing an excellent medium for promoting their new products and industries. So great was the public demand during the 1880s that practically every business — large or small — had cards of one type or another. This method of advertising was actually the beginning of the "brand name" concept of

merchandising, paving the road to success for many companies that are still active today.

Local merchants were the distributors of these cards, and therefore they are more commonly called "trade cards." They were handed to customers, wrapped with a purchase, or simply laid on the counter. Others were given away by salesmen and agents. And there were manufacturers who packed their cards (known as insert cards) within a product, such as cigarettes, gum and candy — as a form of advertising.

Another group is the government postals, which have been extensively used for advertising purposes.

A particularly interesting, attractive, and widely publicized group of cards of the mid-nineteenth century advertised clipper ships. The usual size is 4 x 6½ inches, and since money was plentiful during this period (roughly 1850-1870), no expense was spared in the production of the cards. Their attractive design and bold coloring defies description. Nesbit of New York was the principal printer of these cards, but a few originated elsewhere.

After the discovery of gold in California, there was a tremendous demand for shipping space to carry needed supplies and equipment to the East

"THE OLD OAKEN BUCKET."

Coast. The fastest and best service was provided by the fleet of clipper ships. Since competition was keen, the vessels at first distributed handbills, then attractive sailing cards to customers. These were placed in prominent public places and delivered to prospective shippers. Unfortunately during this period, collecting such cards had not become a general hobby and not many were saved. Nearly 3000 cards are known to exist, and most of these are now in private collections or museums.

Lithographed cards produced by Currier and Ives are very much in demand today. Although their principal output was prints for home decoration, they also did much commercial work such as large banners and store cards. Just prior to 1880 they introduced a line of consumer advertising cards, about 3¼ x 5 inches in size. There were twenty cards each for the cigar trade, the horse and livery trade, and for general advertising. The latter group was later added to.

Most of these cards show the Currier & Ives name, in addition to the copyright date. Because of popular demand, these cards are comparatively scarce and valuable.

Prang issues have a somewhat similar status. Nearly all of his cards are the stock type, with many resembling greeting cards with their bird and flower designs. Most however were originally made for advertising use — and were later adapted to greeting card use. Thus, the same card may often be found with both an advertising and a greeting imprint.

Due to the variety of advertising cards produced, classification has always been rather difficult. However, many collectors divide them into four groups as follows:

1. SPECIAL GROUPS — pre-1850 types, clipper ship cards, Currier & Ives cards, Prang issues.

2. PRODUCT GROUPS — food and beverages, tobacco products, shoes and clothing, personal accessories, farm and business equipment, home furnishings.

3. SERVICE GROUPS — banking, insurance, etc.; transportation; theatrical, amusement, societies; hotels and restaurants.

4. DESIGN GROUPS — art types, and novelties, comics and puzzles, views and portraits, natural history, children's specialties, sports, governmental and racial.

INSERT CARDS

Coffee companies joined the group of insert card issuers during the late 1800s, distributing a number of sets that have become extremely popular with collectors. At that time, all packaged coffee did not have national distribution, therefore these limited area sets are often very elusive. Many are found mixed with early advertising cards in old scrap books. The most desirable cards are those distributed by the Arbuckle Coffee Company, New York City; Woolson Spice Company, Toledo, Ohio (Lion Coffee); McLaughlin Coffee Company, Chicago; Dayton Spice Mills, Dayton, Ohio (Jersey Coffee); International Coffee Company, New York City; and Dilworth's Coffee. Tea cards were also distributed.

Perhaps the most widely distributed group of insert cards were the baking soda cards of Church & Company, John Dwight & Company, and Church & Dwight. The soda cards were distributed from the late 19th Century until the 1920s. The cards pictured beautiful birds, interesting animals — including dogs, fish, colorful flowers, and a Mother Goose Series.

Baker cards were popular in the 1910 period. These were issued with bread and various bakery products, with very few issued on a national basis, making them especially difficult to collect.

Food issues include the ice cream series, in addition to a vast assortment of grocery products of all kinds. Practically every manufacturer of gum and candy issued cards. World War I and sports issues are of special interest to collectors.

Tobacco insert cards were issued with packaged cigarettes as well as cigars. These cards originated in the United States and Canada during the late 1870s as sales promotion devices and subject "enticements." The cards, placed in each pack, reflected such diverse subject matter as Murad's college series, Turkey Red's automobile series, and Hassan's handball players, auto drivers, and swimming champions.

There are also many foreign insert tobacco cards which are worth collecting today.

Fabric inserts of the 1912 period, or the so-called "blankets", are approximately 2½ x 4 inches. Their attractive designs and coloring make them an interesting variant to a card collection. These bulky pieces of tobacco advertising were made of coarse cloth, flannel, silk, or plush. Many have fringed ends. Some have the brand name stamped on the back, but most are unmarked.

DISTRIBUTED BY M. W. HOWARD, DRY GOODS & GROCERIES, NORTH AMHERST, MASS.

SWIFT

In 1855 Gustavus F. Swift borrowed $20 from his father and bought a fat heifer from a Cape Cod neighbor. This was a bold investment for a 16-year-old farm boy, but young Swift knew exactly how to go about making it pay. He dressed the animal in a barn at home. His cuts were so good and his prices so economical that he had no trouble selling the beef to women of the neighborhood. He ended up with a small profit after selling the heifer's hide. From that time he was in business, and became known to his neighbors as "G. F. Swift, dealer in meats."

This was the heifer deal, celebrated in meat packing lore, with which Swift began a career that led to the organization of Swift & Company. On April 1, 1885, the business was incorporated as Swift & Company under the laws of the State of Illinois with a capitalization of $300,000.

PATENTED FEBRUARY 19, 1878

COPYRIGHT 1893

COPYRIGHT 1887   COPYRIGHT 1883

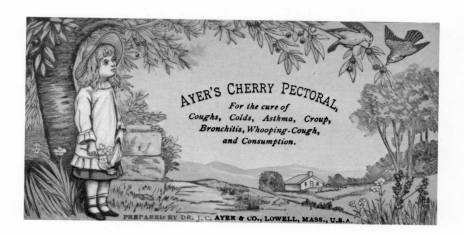

COPYRIGHT 1884

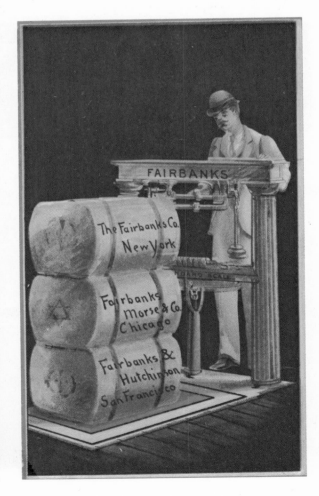

REVERSE STATES: *"For $2.50 you can secure for one year (daily) The Detroit Evening Journal"*

32

Forerunners of today's television commercials

Read Testimonials on other side.

FIRST INTRODUCED, 1833.

MERCHANT'S GARGLING OIL is the standard Liniment of the United States, and is good for Burns, Scalds, Rheumatism, Flesh Wounds, Sprains, Bruises, Lame Back, Hemorrhoids or Piles, Toothache, Sore Throat, Chilblains, Chapped Hands, and many other diseases incident to man and beast. Yellow Wrapper for animal, and white for human flesh.

Manufactured at Lockport, N. Y., by M. G. O. Co., and sold by all druggists.

OVER. JOHN HODGE, Sec'y.

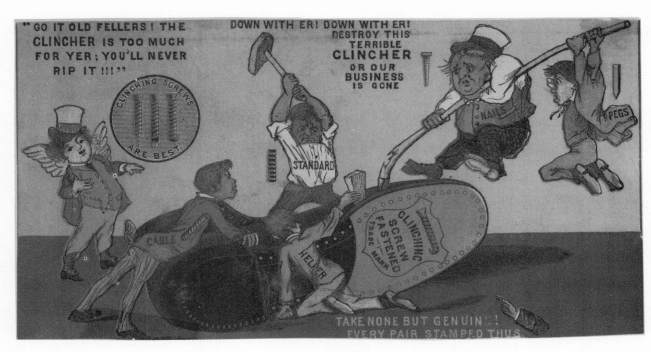

FALSTAFF

Falstaff's rich tradition in brewing dates back to 18th century Germany. There, in the village of Stromberg on a bright winter morning some 200 years ago, a horsedrawn cart clattered over a cobblestone street. The driver pulled on the reins in front of a gabled building, jumped down, and was met at the door by the occupant, a young master brewer by the name of John Henry Griesedieck. Together they loaded the cart with the first barrels of a beer which was new to Stromberg.

The new beer soon met with wide acceptance. John Henry Griesedieck, who had labored long and hard on the formulation and production of his beer, had successfully launched his new career. Falstaff's brewing heritage had begun!

By 1870, several members of the Griesedieck family who were direct descendants of the Stromberg brewer had embarked on brewing careers in St. Louis in America. Joseph Griesedieck, was destined to become the founder of Falstaff Brewing Corporation.

In 1917, despite the shadow of Prohibition looming over the horizon, Joseph Griesedieck scraped together enough money to buy the property and facilities of the Forest Park Brewing Company in St. Louis, and formed his own firm, Griesedieck Beverage Company. The brewery had one 125-barrel brewkettle, and a capacity of barely 10,000 barrels a year. Limited during Prohibition to the production of soft drinks, "near-beer" and even bacon and hams, Griesedieck Beverage Company overcame one financial problem after another during the years following World War I.

During this period the famous Falstaff trademark was acquired from St. Louis' Lemp brewery after it was shut down by Prohibition. The name of the Griesedieck firm then was changed to Falstaff Corporation, and later to Falstaff Brewing Corporation.

At 12:01 a.m. on April 7, 1933, an industry was reborn. Less than a month after repeal the company leased another plant in St. Louis to keep pace with demand for its product. The firm's sales continued to outpace production, and in 1935 Falstaff took the first of its giant strides toward decentralization of production with the acquisition of a brewery in Omaha, Nebraska.

Today, one of the most interesting places for collectors to visit is the Falstaff International Museum of Brewing in St. Louis, Missouri.

Firing the Brew Kettle
1840-1860

The brew kettle was a commonplace fixture in the Adam Lemp Brewery, one of the early St. Louis breweries. A century-old twelve-barrel brew kettle is now on display in the Falstaff International Museum of Brewing.

Aging Beer in Caves
1820-1840

The many caves in St. Louis were ideal for the cool fermentation and storage of lager beer. These caves were an essential factor in the development of St. Louis as a major brewing center.

BUY THE CONQUEROR WRINGER.

WASHING DAY.

THE MARKS' ADJUSTABLE FOLDING CHAIR

OVER
50 CHANGES
Of Position.

A Parlor, Library,
SMOKING, RECLINING,
Or Invalid Chair, Lounge,
FULL LENGTH BED, and
CHILD'S CRIB
Combined in one article.

For Descriptive Catalogue and Price
List, apply to

MARKS' A. F. CHAIR CO. (Lim.)

NEW YORK OFFICE, 850 Broadway.
Two doors above Wallach's Theatre.

over

CHICAGO OFFICE, 234 S. Clark Street,
Grand Pacific Hotel Building.

BUCKEYE FORCE PUMPS.
MAST, FOOS & CO. SPRINGFIELD, O. U.S.A.
AND
34 OLIVER ST., BOSTON, MASS.

MANUFACTURERS OF
LAWN MOWERS,
IRON FENCES,
WIND ENGINES,
ETC. ETC.

38

Bottles

Bottles comprise a vast collecting specialty in themselves, and those that are recognized as important advertising antiques are enormously popular. Actually, it was to a very large extent for the benefit of the manufacturers of bottles that the advertising agency business was established in the United States following the Civil War.

Bottles that once contained bitters, patent medicine, or spirituous liquids are enormously popular. Other types that are of special interest to collectors are those in which any food or personal household product was packed, soft drink bottles, and druggist's bottles.

Old bottles with paper labels are scarce, since there are many enthusiasts who collect this type of label from bottles. Those bottles with embossed lettering always retain their identity as long as the bottle itself survives.

MOLD BLOWN BEER GLASS
1800s

COURTESY BROWN-FORMAN DISTILLERS CORPORATION

THREE RARE "BAR BOTTLES" FROM THE BROWN-FORMAN
LINE AT THE END OF THE 19th CENTURY

39

OLD CROW

Old Crow's beginnings go back to 1825 when a Scottish chemist named James Crow started the experiments that were to elevate whiskey-making from a primitive art to its present standards. Before Dr. Crow came to Woodford County, Kentucky, in 1825, distilling was a backwoods process, a mixing of a "passel" of this and a "passel" of that and then hoping for the best. James Crow, educated in Edinburgh's famed medical university, changed all this. He introduced the saccharometer, the hydrometer, and temperature control to distilling, and developed techniques which produced constantly uniform results.

In 1835 Dr. Crow's studies and experiments came to fruition. He discovered a limestone spring whose pure waters met his every standard of taste and science. Here, at this remote spring on the Kentucky frontier, he built his distillery and put into practice his scientific quality controls. The result was Old Crow.

OLDEST KNOWN BOTTLE OF OLD CROW
COURTESY NATIONAL DISTILLERS PRODUCTS COMPANY

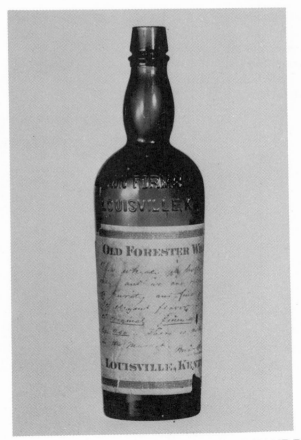

EARLIEST KNOWN OLD FORESTER BOTTLE, HAND BLOWN; DATES FROM THE 1870s, FOUND IN ENGLAND
COURTESY BROWN-FORMAN DISTILLERS CORPORATION

40

EARLY ADVERTISING PIECES — RARE AND COLLECTIBLE
BAR ACCESSORIES AND ADVERTISING NOVELTIES DATING
BACK TO THE 19th CENTURY

FIRST NATIONAL BANK OF CHICAGO
MOST VALUABLE BOTTLE IN THE
BEAM COLLECTION, $1700-$1800

HAROLD'S CLUB OF RENO
BLUE SLOT MACHINE

ST. LOUIS ARCH
GATEWAY TO THE WEST

JAMES B. BEAM

The first Beam distillery was founded in the rolling hills of Kentucky in 1795. The company today is a wholly owned subsidiary of The American Tobacco Company, and at this time there are six members of the Beam family active in management.

Although the Beam company developed colorful containers for their products, it wasn't until 1953 that the company's first specially designed decanter was issued, an appealing glass cocktail shaker.

In 1955 the first Regal China bottles were issued. These were created to deplete an over supply of whiskey.

This was the beginning of a series of many interesting, and immensely popular containers. The bottles, all filled for liquor sale, are never sold empty.

The Executive series was begun in 1955, followed by the Political and Customer specialties in 1956, the Trophy series in 1957, and the State series in 1958.

In 1960 the Beam Company created decanters to commemorate events of historical importance, and this series was known as the "Centennial Series." The first done in this group is the now famous "Santa Fe" bottle, which bears an embossed replica of the Governor's Palace.

In 1966, the Collector's series was introduced.

Of all the Beam bottles produced, the most valuable is the First National Bank of Chicago bottle, which belongs in the Customer Specialty group. Approximately 117 of the bottles were issued. They were given to directors in 1964, to commemorate the 100th anniversery of the bank.

SANTA FE — GOVERNOR'S PALACE

UNUSUAL COLLECTION
OF BEER LABELS

MOLD BLOWN GLASS BEER MUG
1800s

ADVERTISING GLASSES

Advertising glasses are another field of collecting. Today, there is a widespread interest in all types and sizes. Some collectors specialize in soft drink glasses, while others prefer beer glasses with their ornate coats of arms and company emblems with entwining letters and ribbons, which were frequently used as decoration. Those with full illustrations are scarce.

The designs on advertising glasses produced at the turn of the century were almost always a frosty white on clear glass. The message was applied by use of hydrofluoric acid. A band of gold leaf decorated the rims of most glasses during this period.

ANHEUSER-BUSCH, INC.

Anheuser-Busch, Inc., had a very modest beginning four generations ago. It was in 1852 that Eberhard Anheuser became interested in a small brewery and in 1857 acquired control. In 1861, Adolphus Busch, a corporal in the Missouri State Guards during the Civil War, married a daughter of Mr. Anheuser. He became a salesman for his father-in-law and later a partner in the business.

After Mr. Anheuser's death in 1880, Busch took charge of the company. His success was due in large measure to his untiring efforts to brew and distribute the finest beer possible regardless of cost. He applied the then new process of pasteurization which made it possible to ship bottle beer for long distances. With this market advantage, Mr. Busch began to sell his bottle beer throughout the United States. By the end of the 19th century, its production was in excess of one million barrels of beer annually.

It is recorded in an old yearbook, published by S. F. Howe & Co., entitled, "Commercial Manufacturing Interests in St. Louis," that the vast growth of the brewing industry throughout the United States was due in great measure to Adolphus Busch. It states that at the Paris, France, Exposition in 1878, Anheuser-Busch beer was awarded the grand prize over all other breweries in the world.

The feat was acclaimed by a leading Paris newspaper as the most surprising triumph of any American product at the Exposition. The book further states that Anheuser-Busch was the first to build its own icehouses throughout the southern states and first to introduce refrigerator cars to transport beer safely in the hot summer months.

The company enjoys an enviable industry position in other fields. In an effort to survive the prohibition era the company sought to utilize its plant and facilities through diversification in the manufacture of products other than beer. Products of Anheuser-Busch (Industrial Products Division) are bakers yeast, corn syrups, corn starches, dextrines and resins, along with many other affiliated products to the baking industry.

Land acquisition and development is another venture for Anheuser-Busch, Inc. Grant's Farm is an interesting tourist attraction, located just outside St. Louis, on a 281-acre tract which was acquired by the late August A. Busch, Sr., and includes land that was once farmed by Ulysses S. Grant. Grant's Farm is the home of the largest group of Clydesdales in the United States. The horses decorate many of the company's metal serving trays.

FRAMED POSTER — BUDWEISER GIRL
CIRCA 1907

COURTESY ANHEUSER-BUSCH, INC.

OPENERS

Openers that carry advertising are currently collected by hundreds of people, with the figural openers being the most desirable. They often are collected as a category in themselves or as a segment of a broader collection.

BOTTLE OPENER
CIRCA 1880-1890

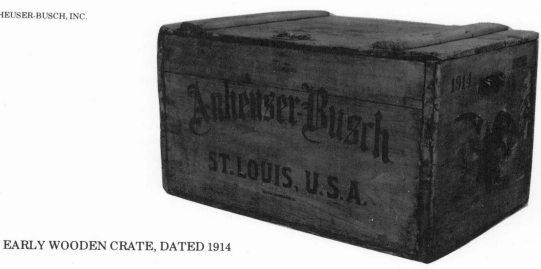

EARLY WOODEN CRATE, DATED 1914

THE ONLY BOTTLE IMITATED! WHY?

DURKEE'S SALAD DRESSING consists only of the very choicest ingredients which long experience and unlimited facilities in obtaining condiments from all over the world can bring together. "Nothing too good" has been the motto.

Just as some people are "covered and not clothed," so most salads are "messed but not dressed." A dash too much of this or a drop too little of that, and the salad is spoiled; and just as the best-fitting clothes are made by those who make a specialty of clothes-making, so the best SALAD DRESSING is made by the house with whom the making of SALAD DRESSING has for years been a study, thus insuring absolute perfection.

Send for FREE booklet on "Salads: How to Make and Dress Them," giving many valuable and novel recipes for Salads, Sandwiches, Sauces, Luncheon Dishes, etc. Sample, 10 cents.

E. R. DURKEE & CO., 543 Washington St., New York

FROM COLLIER'S WEEKLY
June 17, 1899

GLIDDEN-DURKEE

Glidden-Durkee is one of the four largest paint manufacturers in the United States, a major producer of metal powders, one of the largest three spice processors, and one of the largest marketers of olives and pickles.

While Glidden-Durkee, under its former name The Glidden Company, was officially incorporated in 1917, the Glidden name as a factor in American industry traces back to 1870 when Francis H. Glidden started a varnish business in Cleveland under the name of Glidden, Brackett & Company. This was reorganized two years later under the name of The Glidden and Joy Varnish Company, later to become the Glidden Varnish Company in 1883. This operation prospered and a second plant was added in Toronto, Canada. In 1917, Glidden Varnish was purchased by Adrian D. Joyce and a group of his associates, the name being changed to The Glidden Company. Within two years, eleven other manufacturers and distributors of paint and related products were acquired, giving the company manufacturing and distributing facilities in nine states and Canada.

Glidden was a pioneer in corporate diversification and not long after its formation as a paint company was in the pigments and color industry as well. From this business came the company's interest in chemistry which formed the foundation for many of its current businesses including organic and inorganic chemicals, porcelain enamel and ceramic coatings materials, metal powders, and many other products.

In the 1920s, Glidden also entered the food business through the production of edible vegetable oils. This was the forerunner for today's Durkee Famous Foods. The only time in the company's history that there has been a direct relationship between paint and foods was when the company sought ways to use idle machinery designed for crushing flaxseed into linseed oil. It was found that copra could be crushed to yield coconut oil, a leading edible vegetable oil at the time. The experience gained in this venture took Glidden deeper into the edible oil business, and in 1929 the E. R. Durkee & Company was acquired and remains as the leading brand name in Glidden-Durkee's foods organization.

OLD DURKEE BOTTLES DATE BACK TO THE WILD WEST

One of the few products that has survived virtually unchanged from the pioneer days of the Wild West is Durkee's Famous Sauce. Attesting to the longevity of this popular product are the three bottles pictured above. These were found recently in the Huachuca Mountains of Arizona. While it is difficult to trace the exact age of these bottles, they are thought to date from the 1880s. At that time and until 1953, the product was called Durkee's Salad Dressing.

On the largest bottle, the figure of a glove — or gauntlet — can be seen. Before 1929, the company had several lines of products and the Gauntlet was the top quality line. After Glidden acquired the company, this symbol was dropped.

Tobacco Advertising

Europeans were introduced to tobacco in a very unusual manner. When Columbus landed in the West Indies on October 12, 1492, the natives presented him with dried tobacco leaves, one of their prized possessions. Columbus was amazed when he saw Indians of the Caribbean draw smoke through their nostrils from a "Y" shaped pipe they called a "tabaco."

A quarter-century later, a prototype of the cigarette was first seen by Europeans in Mexico, the land of its origin. In 1518, at Yucatan, an Aztec chief gave a reed cigarette to explorer Juan de Grijalva. Described by early historians as "one-and-a-half palms in length," it was a blend of the native tobacco with flavorful herbs, had a recessed mouthpiece, and a charcoal rubbed exterior. This cigarette was an important part of Aztec ceremonial life.

Since suitable reeds were not available to their homeland, the Spaniards developed a paper covering for crushed tobacco similar to our present day cigarette. For several centuries, this way of using tobacco was confined mainly to Spain. Elsewhere on the Continent, pipe-smoking was more popular; however, the cigar had numerous devotees.

Since the lands it conquered in the New World were the sole source of tobacco, Spain virtually controlled the export trade. One of the richest outlets for the leaf called "Spanish" was England.

Through the ingenuity of John Rolfe, the husband of Pocahontas, Spanish tobacco seeds were secured from Venezuela in 1611 — and actually saved Jamestown, Britain's first colony in the New World. Its settlers had founded the colony in the hope of reaping rich rewards from such products as silk, glass, iron, gold, and other items, but these expectations failed.

In desperation they turned to farming and among their export crops to the homeland was tobacco. But once again they ran into obstacles. When smoked the tobacco had a harsh and biting taste. Englishmen, accustomed to the milder and more flavorful leaf from the Spanish colonies, found the Virginia type undesirable.

Rolfe, planted the South American seeds in the rich soil of Virginia, and through crossbreeding and proper curing, the seeds produced a tobacco of exceptional mildness and aroma. Soon it acquired the appropriate name of "sweet-scented." As a result of these improvements, Virginia leaf came into favor, and English importers increased their orders. By 1617, six years after Rolfe's colony-saving deed, Jamestown was exporting 20,000 pounds of leaf yearly.

This thriving new industry financially reinforced the British settlement and gave the mother country a firm hold in the New World. As time went on, the popularity of Virginia tobacco reached the point where it replaced the "Spanish" leaf in British and many European markets. Thus, tobacco became the first basic commodity in the commerce of this country.

The Spanish "cigareet" had universal appeal, and gave to smoking a trim tidiness and compact pleasure. Swiftly, its popularity swept across Europe. In 1850 a German nobleman opened a factory in the Russian capital, St. Petersburg, where he started production of a new kind of cigarette. It was long, had a cotton-type filter, and contained expensive Turkish tobacco. It soon became known as the "Russian-mode," quickly replacing all other types in popularity.

In 1854 British soldiers, engaged in the Crimean War, learned about this cigarette quite by accident. In the course of capturing a group of Russian officers, they casually sampled the Russian cigarettes. The taste for these different cigarettes spread. After the war, vast numbers of the returning British soldiers sought "Russian-mode" cigarettes. Response to this demand marked the start of cigarette manufacturing in England with Robert Gloag, a veteran of the Crimea, opening the first British cigarette factory in 1856. Gloag used a smoke-cured form of Turkish tobacco called "Latakia" for his brand, "Sweet Threes."

During the late 1850s, Philip Morris, Tobacconist & Importer of Fine Seegars, saw a major trend toward cigarettes and capitalized on the sudden popularity. When he went into production, he had a group of expert hand-rollers from Russia, Turkey, and Egypt, turning out highly-prized brands, among them Philip Morris, Cambridge, Oxford Blues, Ovals, and others.

Until about the mid-1800s, the use of tobacco in the United States was limited to snuff, chewing and pipe tobacco. The Mexican war (1846-48) popularized cigars in this country, when troops returned smoking cigarros and cigarillos. Cigarette manufacturing here dates from the Civil War period. One of the earliest "national" brands during the hand-rolling era was Vanity Fair, which was on sale as far west as Chicago during the early 1880s. There was a variety of sizes and shapes, with some cork tips and mouth pieces. The different brands had continental names such as Comme Il Faut, Neapolitan, Polonaises, Militaires, Non Plus, Union Club, Entre Actos, Ultra, Sultana, Havana Imperiales, Jockey Club, Turkish Elegantes, Ladies, Moscows, Uncle Sam, No Name 10s, No Name 24s, Petit Canons, Operas, and St. Petersburg.

During the 1870s, six manufacturing firms controlled seventy-five percent of the expanding cigarette market, employing experienced immigrant rollers. Kimball of Rochester manufactured Vanity Fair, Cloth of Gold, Fragrant Vanity Fair, Three Kings, Turkish Orientals and Old Golds. Marburg of Baltimore had Estrella, Golden Age, and High Life. Kinney of New York had Full Dress, Halves, Kinney's Sweet Caporal, Sportsman's Caporal, Caporals, and Kinney's Straight Cut. Allen & Ginter of Richmond had Our Little Beauties, Richmond Gem, Richmond Straight Cut No. 1, Bon Tons, Napoleons and Opera Puffs. Goodwin of New York had Old Judge, Welcome, and Canvas Back.

By the close of the last century, the fad for cigarettes seemed to be doomed because of the federal tax, which had tripled between the years 1897 and 1898, completely extinguishing many of the nickel brands. The result was a fifty percent decrease in cigarette smoking between 1896 and 1901. During the following year, however, the government lowered taxes almost to the 1896 level, and the cigarette smoking boom was on.

The following dates and information will be of special interest to collectors in this field — considered by many to be the leading field of advertising collectibles.

1890 — peak of chewing tobacco consumption in the United States.
1907 — peak of cigar consumption in United States.
1921 — cigarettes were the leading form of tobacco consumption.

Unfortunately, space does not permit a comprehensive list of every brand of tobacco and the date it was introduced. Therefore, the authors suggest the following books:

TOBACCO AND AMERICANS — Robert K. Heimann, 1960.
THE MIGHTY LEAF — J. E. Brooks, 1952.
THE STORY OF TOBACCO IN AMERICA — J. C. Robert, 1949.

"LIBERTY" — PINE PAINTED FIGURE
CIRCA 1875

CIGAR STORE FIGURES

The story of the tobacco trade can almost be told in the evolution of the cigar store figures, as they symbolized the enchantment of faraway lands.

The first known wooden Indians were those of London which appeared shortly after the first commercial shipment of leaf. These characters were not American Indians, but black men in feather headdresses and girdles of tobacco leaves. It wasn't until about 1840 that the true likeness of the American Indian became common in American cities east of the Mississippi. By this time most of the redskins were being deported west of that river into Indian Territory.

These silent salesmen were very eye-catching to the passersby, then as now. At one time there were over 100,000 of them, but there are few survivors. Some tobacconists in the larger cities chained their wooden Indians to outside walls, while others had their Indians placed onto small platforms so that they could be wheeled into the shops at nightfall. After the Civil War, many figures were cast in metal.

At this time the wholesale multiplication of different brands was accompanied by a widened variety of shop statues, such as buckskinned pioneers and trappers, cavaliers, ladies of fashion, sailors, minstrel characters, historical figures like Raleigh or Washington, baseball players, and a beckoning Punch with a fat paunch and leer to match. The latter was one of the most popular types. However, nine out of every ten were still Indians — peering braves or Pocahontases.

The great majority of cigar store Indians carved in the United States between 1840 and 1890, held a bunch of wooden cigars. Now and then in the hands of a wooden baseball player a bat replaced the cigars. Many of the Indian figures were made to hold a dagger, musket, or tomahawk. The so-called "Longfellow Indian," (greatly admired by Longfellow who had written "Hiawatha" in 1855), held a bow and arrow.

FIGURES COURTESY HENRY FORD MUSEUM

50

CIGAR BANDS AND LABELS

Cigar bands are a type of label collected since their origin about 1854. The size and ornateness of the bands vary greatly. Those that are oversized should really be called "wrappers" because they were designed to go around several cigars — perhaps as many as a dozen. Most of these large examples are beautiful.

Manufacturers have long had a custom of naming their cigars after prominent people. Commemorative bands which were made for such brands are considered the most desirable, especially those with portraits shown. The foreign cigar bands are often considered superior to locals in design and coloring.

The souvenir bands were made only to sell to collectors, thus none have actually been used on cigars. They are usually in sets, showing Presidents, decks of cards, the alphabet, etc.

Many of the bands have unusual names, especially those that have been named for thoroughbred race horses, since the name is retired with the horse and cannot be used again. But, some of the early cigar makers exercised a great deal of imagination and came up with some very unusual names such as Some Smoke, Safety Smoke, Seal Skin, Pow Wow, All Aces, El Weezo, Juicy, The Bulldog, and Conquering Cupid.

The above are just a few of the strange names that have appeared on cigar bands. In addition, there were bands made for hotels, insurance companies, banks, senators, authors, artists, actors, and territories now long vanished. Many of these are heavy with gilt and exquisitely engraved. And the different treatment of monarchs such as Edward VII is very interesting.

Collecting colorful and interesting old cigar bands is on the upsurge. Compared with other collectible objects today, they are fairly inexpensive — except for the rarities.

Cigar box labels are also of interest to the collector of tobacco mementos. Some of the brands had a very brief lifetime, while others have been on the market for scores of years. The printing and selling of box labels has been an extensive business with several firms, and there are catalogs showing samples of their work and stock designs available to any manufacturer.

These labels were produced at a very early date. Those labels dating before 1880 are especially desirable. However, they must show a date — usually in a copyright notice.

"SENECA JOHN" CARVED BY ARNOLD AND PETER RUEF, TIFFIN, OHIO — 1880s — HEIGHT 7'3"

51

*cigar
bands*

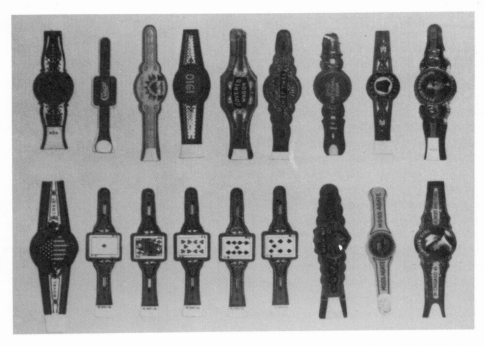

ALL CIGAR BANDS COURTESY MRS. KAY ARCHER

*early
tobacco posters*

TIN TOBACCO TAGS

Tin tobacco tags were originated by George Lorillard, famed tobacco manufacturer and promoter. The idea caught on quickly, and soon every brand had its distinctive design. The paper labels were fastened to the plug by the teeth of the tin tag. There are two types of tin tobacco tags, plain embossed and colored enamel. A large collection will include from 4,000 to 5,000 tags.

The tags served two purposes: they prolonged the plug, and they constituted a trademark identification and some assurance of consistent quality. In addition, they were also recognized as premium tokens, redeemable for prizes and cash.

Around the turn of the present century, the R. J. Reynolds Tobacco Company issued small 3 x 5 inch illustrated catalogs of presents given for tobacco tags. These interesting little books offered dozens of items such as furniture, jewelry, dishes, guns, clothing, etc. Some of the tags were worth as much as half a cent a piece in trade-in value, although one-eighth of a cent was closer to the average. These small books are sought after by collectors as they should form a part of every good tobacco tag collection.

Resembling coins in size — and sometimes in shape — the tags were as original in both design and wording as the cigar bands of the day. Colors were profuse in bright red, green, and gold. Among the hundreds of designs were tags shaped as apples, barrels, spoons, sickles, men's boots, the bottom of a shoe, Maltese Cross, hammers, flat irons, trowels, and ship's wheel. Some tags appeared merely as capital letters, while others were large-sized numbers.

Alto chewing tobacco was identified with tin tags cut out to resemble animals such as horses, cattle, elephants, camels, plus ALTO prominently lettered thereon. These proved to be excellent trade name advertising.

The first chewing tobacco was distributed in bulk, making it difficult to handle. However, the pressed cut plug was a well-seasoned and "sweetened" chaw tobacco. Manufacturers spiced it with rum, molasses, sugar, and syrups. These tasty ingredients led to tin tags announcing Sweet Skylight, Hunk o' Honey, Lilac Taste, Sweet Tooth (shaped like a tooth), Champagne Chaw, Old Varginy, and Sweet Isaac.

It has often been said that cigars left a heritage of brilliant paper bands, while pipes left a trail of handsome, hand-carved bowls, but chewing tobacco left its imprint with the tin tag.

ALL TOBACCO TAGS COURTESY HENRY GRIFFEN

53

54

Every day thousands of Americans fill their pipes from familiar red tins that feature the picture of a bearded man in a frock coat. The product is Prince Albert, manufactured by the R. J. Reynolds Tobacco Company.

Prince Albert played a major role in the early growth of Richard Joshua Reynolds' tobacco business because it marked a new departure in his career. Before Mr. Reynolds introduced the brand in 1907, his company's main product was plug tobacco. But he had a determination to produce a smoking tobacco that could catch the eye and smoking taste of the public. One of his first steps was to associate the name of the tobacco with a man who was, at that time, in the public's eye.

At the time the new smoking tobacco was being developed, many distinguished men were wearing a stylish frock coat, called "Prince Albert" for a young prince of the British ruling family, Albert Edward, eldest son of Queen Victoria.

Prince Albert had worn his frock coat when he visited the United States on a well publicized tour. When his mother, Queen Victoria, died in 1901, he ascended to the throne of England as King Edward VII.

With a solid idea for a brand name Mr. Reynolds designed a label for the tobacco which was to become tops in the industry. He used the picture of King Edward in a "Prince Albert" coat.

For the product he had named Prince Albert, Reynolds selected a long burning, crimp cut tobacco blend. A patent on the now famous blend was granted July 30, 1907.

When the brand was first placed on the market in August, 1907, it was packed in red cloth bags that sold for five cents each. Prince Albert's name and picture were prominently displayed on each bag. Later the same year the tobacco was marketed in tins.

In 1909 Reynolds began producing its own Prince Albert tins at what is now No. 9 Metal Can Department. Even today the company is the only smoking tobacco manufacturer making its own tins.

When the company's red tins were introduced they carried this statement: "PRINCE ALBERT tobacco is prepared for smokers under the process discovered in making experiments to produce the most delightful and wholesome tobacco for cigarette and pipe smokers — PATENTED PROCESS July 30, 1907."

When a new package design was introduced in

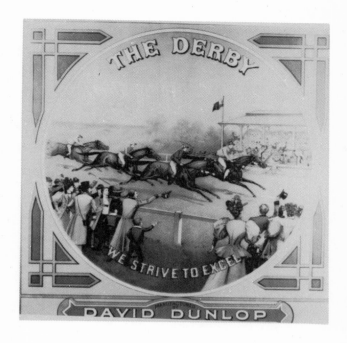

1960, this statement was not included. But the picture of Queen Victoria's bearded balding son in the long frock coat remained, continuing the tradition Reynolds had started 53 years before. It should be noted here that the company introduced PRINCE ALBERT in a foil pouch the same year.

According to company records, the much sought after George Washington "lunchbox" tin was used between the years 1913 and 1931; the metal container for Camel "flat-fifties" from January, 1930, until about 1940; the oval tin container from July 15, 1953, until March 13, 1956, for Cavalier cigarettes (a brand discontinued in 1968).

MATCH LABELS

Match labels were originally the thin paper pasted on the small wood (later cardboard) box. Most originated in Japan and Scandinavia — and make an attractive collection when grouped.

Today, the box type has been largely supplanted by the folders, and the vast bulk of these little folders are of a purely advertising nature.

Trays

Colorful, lithographed, tin advertising trays, and art plates are enjoying great popularity today; thus prices have risen in a spectacular manner during the past few years. These mementos are reminders of a once quaint and elegant time in our history — hence, nostalgia has created their skyrocketing popularity.

Trays generally fall into two categories in so far as size is concerned. The larger serving trays were made in round, rectangular, and oval shapes, ranging in sizes from 9¾ inches, to 25 inches. The larger sizes are quite rare, and these were primarily used as wall decorations for saloons.

The miniature trays, sometimes called "tip" or "change" trays, were usually placed by the cash register, or on the fountain or bar. They are ordinarily found in round 4½ to 6 inch sizes, or in oval or rectangular shapes.

Art plates, approximately 10 inches in diameter, were always round and quite ornate. They were made in limited quantities, therefore a popular demand has made them scarce and valuable. The advertising imprinted on them was in small lettering, rather than in the usual prominent style of the larger trays. The Coca-Cola Company issued several outstanding examples.

The advertising trays — large or small — were used commercially for almost all types of businesses. Breweries and soft-drink bottlers had the greatest number and variety. However, not all trays are bottle-related. There were trays to advertise ice cream, clothing, flour, soap, cigars, coffee, watches, bakeries, dairies, grocers, confectionaries, separators, insurance companies, and mail order firms. Whiskey trays were also issued but they are scarce.

It is relatively easy to estimate the age of a tray as most manufacturers identified themselves in microscopic lettering in an inconspicuous area on the face of the tray, and in many instances the date of the copyright is also included.

The history of the tin advertising tray begins during the 1880s in Coshocton, Ohio. The idea of novelty advertising was conceived by two competing Coshocton newspapermen, J. F. Meek and H. D.

COURTESY KEN BASSETT

Beach. Occasionally another local printer, William Shaw, is credited with this interesting type of advertising.

In 1887 Meek began printing colorful ads on burlap school bags, and his new concept of advertising was an immediate success. Other novelties were quickly added to the line, including grocery aprons, newspaper bags, fans, and even backs of chairs. He named his new enterprise The Tuscarora Advertising Company.

The following year, Beach organized The Standard Advertising Company and began producing novelty advertising items, including the first 12-sheet commercial advertising calendar in 1889.

Around 1890 Beach began using steam power presses, which enabled him to print directly on enameled metal, and in 1895 Meek's firm succumbed to the metal phase of printing. They were the first company to use this new method of printing on metal in a commercial way. Early trays and signs bearing the name Tuscarora date from 1895 to 1901, when the two rival Coshocton companies merged as the Meek and Beach Company in March of that year. In October 1901 Beach withdrew and organized his own firm, which was known as The H. D. Beach Company and is still active today. Meek continued in business, using the name Meek and Beach Company until 1905, when he changed to the Meek Company. The firm prospered and in 1909 was reorganized and named the American Art Works Company. They produced many of the early Coca-Cola trays. The firm continued to make trays, signs, and other advertising novelties until 1950, when operations ceased.

Another well known manufacturer of lithographed advertising trays was Kaufmann & Strauss, New York City. This firm was organized in 1890 and was active in producing metal signs, as well as other advertising specialties, well into the present century.

Other lithographing companies that produced metal trays were Bachrach Company, San Francisco, California, 1895-1918; Schonk and Company, Chicago, Illinois, 1890-1930s; and The American Colortype Company, Newark, New York. This firm was incorporated by the American Art Works in 1930. The American Can Company also made trays. However, their name does not appear on early issues — only on trays of more recent origin.

Although most of the larger companies had their trays custom made, a larger percentage of the trays found today are "stock" designs, which were made available to any company that wanted to imprint the company name on the tray. The design in general had no relation to the product. These trays were sold to anyone who cared to use them.

Subject material for trays varied widely. Ornamented and colorful company emblems, trademarks, or a factory view decorated many trays. Outdoor scenes were frequently used to attract sportsmen, and animals were also a popular subject. The male figure on early advertising trays is scarce, while children seemed to be a favorite subject, especially of the ice cream trade. The most eagerly sought after trays today are those that were decorated primarily for the male drinking contingent, which feature lightly clad beauties. The popular Coca-Cola trays and art plates that feature the topless girls were used in bars and taverns in the Chicago area between and including the years of 1908 and 1912.

Early advertising trays, regardless of size or shape, and art plates, are of great interest to collectors nowadays, as well as decorators. They are very appealing when used as wall decoration in an office, recreation room or a Gay Nineties type restaurant.

TRAYS BOTH PAGES
COURTESY KEN BASSETT

WORLD WAR I GIRL — 1917

LILLIAN NORDICA (1903)
CANADIAN REPRODUCTION — 1969
HUTCHISON-STYLE BOTTLE
STRAIGHT-WALLED GLASS IN METAL HOLDER

COCA-COLA

John Styth Pemberton, the originator of Coca-Cola, was born in Knoxville, Georgia, in 1833. He grew up in Columbus and obtained a degree in pharmacy at Macon, Georgia.

Always curious and in search of something new in mixtures of flavors for pharmaceutical products, Pemberton hit on the idea of a palatable soft drink that would be distinctive in taste and which could be sold over the soda fountain. Records do not reveal when the soft-drink idea was conceived, but it was probably about 1880.

One day in May, Pemberton drew off a quantity of a reddish brown syrup and took it to Willis Venable's fountain in Jacobs' drug store. Venable was acknowledged as the "soda-water king" of Atlanta.

Pemberton showed Venable the syrup, and asked him to draw off an ounce of it, mix the syrup in a glass with some ice and carbonation and try its taste. This Venable did and was so pleased that he agreed to dispense the new beverage at his soda fountain on a trial basis.

Although Venable's customers were interested in the new product known as Coca-Cola, there was no general public acceptance of the drink. Actually, as the months went by it looked like the new beverage was headed for oblivion. However, Pemberton was determined to put the product over, despite his own failing health. In the first year from June, 1886, to June, 1887, he was able to sell only 25 gallons of the syrup, while piling up an advertising cost of $46.

Pemberton's first advertising consisted of signs, painted on oilcloth and fastened to drug store awnings by pins. The signs bore the simple invitation to "Drink Coca-Cola 5¢." Unfortunately, none of these first point-of-sale signs are known to exist.

Finally, Dr. Pemberton's health became so bad he considered it necessary to get away from business entirely. From that point on, the good will, the formula, and the trademark changed hands several times, until 1891 when Asa G. Candler acquired 100 percent interest in Coca-Cola. Candler, an Atlanta wholesale druggist, sold his drug business in order to devote full time to the manufacture and sale of the beverage.

The business was incorporated on January 29, 1892, as "The Coca-Cola Company," a Georgia corporation, with capital stock of $100,000.

The first advertising budget of the new corporation provided $11,401.78 for the year. Since that time, the name Coca-Cola has been reproduced on glass, porcelain, tin, fiber, gold, silver, plastic, card-board, marble, paper, stainless steel, bone, wood, ivory, cloth, copper, and brass. It has been printed, lithographed, painted, and written in the sky.

To advertise his product Candler began painting walls. He put up signs in the form of a 30-foot-high glass of Coca-Cola in ball parks, and to get people to try his new product, gave out colorfully lithographed cards — good for one free drink of Coca-Cola at a soda fountain.

Coca-Cola was first bottled in 1894, when a Vicksburg, Mississippi, man put it up for lumbermill gangs and isolated plantations.

In 1899, the large scale bottling of Coca-Cola was made possible by contract between The Coca-Cola Company and Benjamin F. Thomas and Joseph B. Whitehead, both of Chattanooga, Tennessee.

Those who know the history of Coca-Cola know that without the keen business insight and executive ability of Candler, it would never have become any-thing more than one of a thousand other proprietary products developed but allowed to struggle and die.

During the "Gay Nineties," The Coca-Cola Com-pany made a remarkable growth; and during this period many promotional items were introduced, such as calendars, trays, clocks and urns.

The earliest calendar of which the company has record was issued by Candler in 1891. Presumably calendars were issued annually by the company. However, a number of issues in the Nineties have never been found, along with the issues of 1905 and 1906.

All of the early calendars for Coca-Cola were colorful, featuring lovely ladies. While the "pretty girl" predominated, there have been variations, including flower arrangements and birds. The most notable series is the Norman Rockwell pictures which appeared on the calendars during the late 1920s and early 1930s. Santa Claus has been featured on every December calendar since 1930.

Lithographed metal serving and change trays were introduced during the early 1890s. They came in round, rectangular, square, and oval shapes.

Clocks and urns were used for advertising Coca-Cola about 1896. The urns were white, with gold trim and red lettering. These usually stood on the foun-tain or back-bar. The top (covered by a lid) held one gallon of Coca-Cola syrup. With a handle below, the soda clerk was able to dispense an ounce of the syrup into a glass. The urns were used for about ten years.

One of the most sought-after items made available to retail establishments was the stained glass leaded chandelier. These came in two basic back-ground colors, red and green, with the trademark Coca-Cola in white.

TRADE MARK — NO DATE

AUMUMN GIRL — 1922
FLARED GLASS

PICNIC BASKET WAGON — TELEVISION TRAY — 1958

SUMMER GIRL — 1921
FLARED GLASS

CURB SERVICE — 1927

Other advertising collectibles for Coca-Cola used during the first quarter of the present century are Japanese fans, door plates, and handles, pocket knives, hats, aprons, blotters, caps, wagon umbrellas, book matches, oval mirrors, cuff links, sewing kits, thermometers, watch fobs, leather and celluloid bookmarks, brass door knobs, marble paperweights, wallets, change purses, openers, ice picks, card cases, thimbles, "Little Gem" dictionaries, nature study cards featuring birds and insects, and various types of informative booklets.

During the mid-1920s The Coca-Cola Company became interested in coolers. One of the most popular was a syrup barrel cut in half — and another interesting type was the wooden ice box with a sliding lid.

The first automatic fountain dispenser was developed in 1932. It became increasingly popular and represented a long step forward in the serving of a uniform, properly refrigerated product at the fountain.

The early Coca-Cola bottles are much sought after by collectors. By 1909 there were 374 bottlers of Coca-Cola in the United States, using the embossed, straight-sided glass bottles. Colors included Georgia green, light blue, clear, and amber. Sizes and shapes were determined by the bottler — some were tall, some squat, some contained six ounces, others six and one-half and seven ounces.

The universally known bottle was designed by Alexander Samuelson in 1915. Often called "The Grande Dame," the bottle was designed to resemble the hobble skirts that women wore at that time. Samuelson patented his design in November, and the new "hobble skirt" bottle went into production in 1916. For the first years the bottle was manufactured solely by the Root Glass Company. For seven years, the design of the bottle went unchanged, then in 1923 Root took over the patent from Samuelson, and the patent date appearing on the side of the bottle became "Dec. 25, 1923." Since the U.S. Patent Office always issued patents on Tuesday, even when not open for business, this bottle has become known as the "Xmas Bottle."

Embossed on the bottom of all "hobble-skirt" bottles produced from 1916 to 1955 is the geographical location of the owning plant. In 1955, The Coca-Cola Company deleted the embossing on the bottom of the bottles and adopted the "Applied Color Label" in white lettering. Ten years later the policy of embossing the city and bottler on the bottom of the bottles was readopted.

The story of Coca-Cola continues to unfold each year — maintaining the status of the most heavily advertised product in the world.

LILLIAN RUSSELL — 1904

GIRL WITH BOBBED HAIR — 1928

TWENTIES SPORTS COUPLE — 1926

FARM BOY — 1931

1915

1905

1916

COURTESY JACK AND GLORIA MUZIO
PHOTOS BY CHRIS MANNION

JOSEPH SCHLITZ BREWING COMPANY

The Joseph Schlitz Brewing Company has been producing "The Beer That Made Milwaukee Famous" for 125 years. The company was founded in Milwaukee in 1849 by August Krug, a German immigrant, and is still owned and operated today by his direct descendants. Brewing in Krug's day was a small business operation. Many families brewed their own beer, and there were literally thousands of small breweries in the nation. So, when Krug's brewery increased its first year production of 150 barrels to 250 barrels in 1850, he was quite elated. Yet, it hardly was an augury of the tremendous popularity that was to come.

In 1850, August Krug hired Joseph Schlitz, a young man of 20, to be his bookkeeper. That same year Krug also brought his eight-year-old nephew, August Uihlein, from Germany to live with him. Krug died in 1856 and Schlitz assumed management of the brewery. Some time later he married Krug's widow. The brewing company took the Schlitz name in 1874. A year later, Schlitz was lost at sea when the Steamer Schiller went down in the Irish Sea. Management of the brewery passed to August Uihlein and his three brothers, Henry, Alfred, and Edward. Robert A. Uihlein, Jr., president and board chairman of the brewery today, is a grandson of August. Although the Joseph Schlitz Brewing Company is one of the few major American firms still operated by direct decendants of the founder, stock in the company is publicly held.

One of the first milestones in the growth of the Schlitz company is connected with the great Chicago fire of 1871, a disaster which left the city low on water. The Schlitz company shipped in barrels and barrels of beer for the beleaguered citizens of Chicago. They liked the product from the brewery in Milwaukee, and kept on drinking it when things returned to normal. That was the start of the growth of the Schlitz company from a local industry to the present network of breweries. It also inspired one of the most famous merchandising slogans in the world, "The Beer That Made Milwaukee Famous."

Today, Schlitz markets four brands of beer: Schlitz, Old Milwaukee; Primo, a Hawaiian brand; Encore, recently introduced — plus Schlitz Malt Liquor.

Left, top to bottom: Sunburst tray, metal lithograph, Lemp Brewery, early 1900s; Trademark tray, metal lithograph, American Brewery, St. Louis, early 1900s; Pabst Brewing Company tray, metal lithograph, produced after Repeal, 1933.

Center, top to bottom: Sir John Falstaff, metal lithograph tray, Falstaff Brewing Corporation, 1940s; National Brewery metal lithograph tray, pictures brewery and product, 1890s.

Right, top to bottom: White sunburst tray, metal lithograph, Lemp Brewery, early 1900s; Metal lithograph tray, pictures Louis Obert and Louis Obert Brewery, St. Louis, early 1900s; Metal lithograph tray pictures serving maid, classic art work, Fecker Brewery, Danville, Illinois, early 1910.

1908

1910-1915

1900-1910

1913

COURTESY JACK AND GLORIA MUZIO
PHOTOS BY CHRIS MANNION

68

THREE CHANGE TRAYS

MILLER BREWING COMPANY

Frederic Miller came from Germany in 1855 and bought a small brewery on a site then far west, namely Milwaukee. He named it Frederic Miller's Plank-Road Brewery.

His genius was exhibited in many ways. Once when plagued with a shortage of space in which to store his famous beer, he solved the problem by digging caves in a hill beside the plant. Hand dug and lined with brick and limestone to prevent seepage of water, the caves are still in use.

With Prohibition the Miller family lost its usual market and sought to branch out into new products, such as cereal beverage, malt tonic, health drink, malt syrup and carbonated soft drinks under the Miller label.

The end of Prohibition in 1933 marked the beginning of a new era at Miller. With its beer again available to a receptive public, the brewery took stock of itself. A program of modernization and expansion was begun, but the company was determined to maintain the quality standards that Miller High Life was famous for.

When Frederic A. Miller died in 1947, his nephew, Frederic C. Miller, took over the post of president. The new chief executive carried out a tremendous expansion program which turned Miller Brewing Company into one of the world's most modern breweries. Miller and his son Fred, Jr., died in a plane crash in Milwaukee in December, 1954.

In 1965, controlling interest in the company was bought by W. R. Grace & Company. Charles W. Miller, formerly group vice-president for Grace, became the new president.

The acquisition of Miller Brewing Company by Philip Morris Incorporated in June, 1969, has brought a major addition to this diversified, international, multi-product corporation.

1908

COURTESY KEN BASSETT

THE PABST BREWING COMPANY

In 1842 Jacob Best, Jr., and Charles Best established a vinegar factory in Milwaukee, Wisconsin. Two years later, Charles returned to Mettenheim, Germany, and brought the rest of the Best family to Milwaukee. On September 10 of that year, the first real estate was purchased on Chestnut Street Hill, the present site of the Pabst Brewing Company.

The brewery, Best and Company, was owned and operated by Jacob Best, Sr., and his sons, Jacob, Jr., Charles, Philip, and Lorenz.

In 1845, the first lager beer from Best and Company was made available for sale, and on July 1, 1852, the first display advertisement for Best and Company was placed in the *Wisconsin Banner*.

Frederick Pabst came to America from Germany in 1848, and on March 25, 1862, he married Philip Best's daughter, Maria. Two years later Best took Captain Pabst into business as an equal partner. When Best's daughter, Elizabetha, married Emil Schandein, the partnership between Philip Best and Captain Pabst was dissolved, and a new partnership agreement between Pabst and Emil Schandein was drawn up for Best and Company.

On March 13, 1873, the company was incorporated. It started bottling in 1875. Three years later Best beer was awarded a gold medal at the World's Fair in Paris, and in 1889 the name of the company was changed to Pabst Brewing Company.

The words "Blue Ribbon" were added to the label of "Select" beer in 1895, and in January 1898 the Blue Ribbon label was first used. This change was well received and given favorable publicity.

Magazine and newspaper advertising was undertaken around the turn of the century. Also included were fancy calendars, notices in railroad timetables, and theater programs. Matchboxes, souvenir cigar cases, memorandum pads, and New Year's cards with the name "Pabst" brightly displayed were distributed. Indoor and outdoor signs and pictures were given to retailers, agents and saloons carrying Pabst. Starting in 1903, illustrations included a picture of the brewery, and a picture of two Blue Ribbon bottles on a table with a glass of beer and a plate of oysters on the half shell. This picture became almost as famous in the history of early 20th century display advertising as the Victor Talking Machine Company's "His Master's Voice."

ADMIRAL DEWEY TRAY (RARE)
DATED 1900

TRAYS BOTH PAGES
COURTESY KEN BASSETT

Signs of the Times

Early store signs, posters, banners, as well as elegant paper or tin lithographed signs, are eagerly collected today. Later examples, such as the Grape-Nuts Girl and Her St. Bernard, with an embossed tin frame, are especially rare and valued.

During the horse-and-buggy days stores displayed trade signs of every conceivable shape — either above their doors or on the sidewalks before them. This is the silent group of trade signs, as their very existence was sufficient to inform anyone that here was a particular kind of business. A big hat signified the hat manufacturer, while a giant pair of glasses indicated the optical supply manufacturer. The jeweler displayed a large dummy clock, the pharmacist a mortar and pestle, the barber a colorful striped barber pole, and the cigar store a wooden Indian.

By the Civil War a considerable proportion of the trade signs were standardized and mass-produced. In most instances, a merchant simply ordered the desired trade sign from a catalog supplied by wholesale manufacturers who carried them in stock.

Around the turn of the century, when radio and television was still unheard of, the interiors of stores were used for poster, banner, and picture advertising to attract the public. The tobacco firms were prolific advertisers, using a constant procession of banners. The large signs were an ever-changing attraction for customers, and attractive framed pictures were prized. Since window trimming had not been developed at that time, many of the above signs were hung in windows.

Finally, it should be noted here that early ads that include an American flag, or a negro, are of added value because they are desired by collectors, and known brand names are also of greater value.

MOVIE POSTERS

Old handbills, broadsides, movie and circus posters are becoming more and more collectible. Many of the early colored posters vividly displayed the known — or not-so-well-known — stars of the stage, screen and roadshows. The posters had litho-

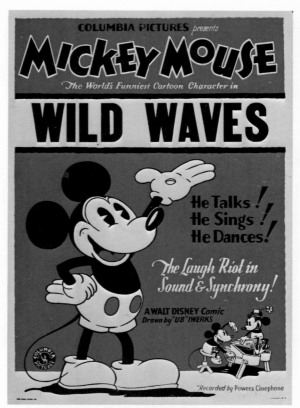

RELEASED DECEMBER 21, 1929

RELEASED APRIL 30, 1931

COURTESY ©WALT DISNEY PRODUCTIONS

73

reproduced posters

COURTESY FERRY-MORSE SEED COMPANY

graphed scenes suitable for such shows as circus, carnival, singers, dancers, dog and pony, magic, vaudeville, mind reading, and rodeo.

The old Laurel and Hardy posters are enjoying much popularity now, in addition to those depicting Walt Disney's first animated character, Mickey Mouse, along with Donald Duck, Pluto, the Three Little Pigs, and many others.

Collectors of the 1930 Disney posters illustrated here are increasing in number each year.

Values for the above items vary greatly, depending upon uniqueness, scarcity and condition.

SODA POP

The soft drink industry is a typically American development. We consume nearly 200 bottles per capita. Carbonated beverages is the preferred term. The word "soda" dates back to the late 1700s vogue for artificial mineral waters in which "fossil alkali" or bicarbonate of soda, was mixed with pure water. Mentioned in the first Pharmacopoeia of the United States in 1820, soda water soon after became "carbonic acid water" when the bicarb was supplanted by carbon dioxide as the fizz agent. We still call it "soda."

To the digust of the trade, we also call it "pop." And while this sounds like a modern teenage term, it really originated in Civil War times. Quite naturally, it evolved from the explosive noise made when the cork was withdrawn from the bottle or jug.

The early bottles had a rubber stopper which remained in the bottle at all times. It was attached to a wire hook which was used to pull the stopper up into the neck of the bottle after it had been filled. The pressure of the carbonated water kept the stopper tight. When the bottle was filled, the wire hook extended above the neck of the bottle. To open, you simply hit the hook firmly, pushing the rubber stopper down.

Since Colonial days, millions of corks have unexpectedly popped from such bottles, for the soft drink business started as a kitchen craft, or a do-it-yourself activity. Largely to combat the appeal of intoxicating beverages in a lusty era when the real Spirit of '76 was rum, contemporary housewives concocted a wide assortment of "herb teas," mostly using roots, barks, berries and herbs. Sarsaparilla, Birch Beer and Nettle Beer were very popular. Switchel, containing molasses, vinegar, and ginger in water, was an old-time favorite. So was Ginger Beer, Spruce Beer and Persian Mead. These could be fermented to a mild two to four percent alcoholic content, depending upon the aging. Mead, which was widely favored, was made with honey, yeast, sugar and water, flavored with oil of nutmeg or wintergreen. Spruce Beer was such a staple that Washington's army got a ration of a quart a day.

While this home brewing of soft and semi-soft beverages flourished for well over a century, physicians and chemists were giving their attention chiefly to the bottling of artificial mineral waters, Balston, Saratoga, Vichy, Seltzer, and others. In time, the apothecaries got into the act. In 1815 they introduced a number of prepared powders for the making of synthetic mineral waters at home. A few years later, the first soda fountain was patented by Samuel Fahenstock of Lancaster, Pennsylvania. The era of palatable, fruit-flavored soft drinks, as contrasted to medicinal potions, got under way. Some of the early flavors rarely heard of today included Mulberry, Barberry, Gooseberry, Currant, Checkerberry, and Cranberry.

Some unknown druggist hit on the idea of adding sweet cream to the fruit syrup and charged water, giving birth to the "Iced Cream Soda." But it wasn't until 1874, during the Franklin Institute's Semi-Centennial Exposition in Philadelphia, that the "d" was dropped from the word "iced." This happened when a soda fountain operator at the Exposition suddenly ran out of sweet cream at the peak of the rush. He hurriedly sent out to a nearby confectioner's for a supply of ice cream which he planned to melt. But the thirsty throng couldn't wait, so he plopped the frozen ice cream into the sodas — and another 100 percent American beverage went into orbit.

In 1885, Dr. Pepper was put on the market, and in 1886, Coca-Cola was created and first sold in Atlanta, Georgia.

In 1885 Moxie appeared on the market in Boston, and White Rock made its bow. By August 28, 1898, young Caleb D. Bradham (pharmacist) had given the name of his own creation "Pepsi-Cola."

HIRE'S ROOT BEER

Despite these stirrings of an infant industry, it was the housewife and the pharmacist who still dominated the soft drink field through the 19th century. And it was a happy coalition of these two elements — plus a wily touch from a clergyman — that put Hires Root Beer on the market.

In 1869, young Charles E. Hires quit a $1-a-week job as an apothecary's apprentice in Millville, New Jersey, and moved to Philadelphia. Getting a job in a drug store there, he attended night classes at the Philadelphia College of Pharmacy and the Jefferson Medical School. When he had saved up $400 he

1920s SIGN

VINTAGE POSTER

FRAMED POSTER

CARDBOARD SIGN
COURTESY LAVERNE AND JENNY REINERT

rented a small drug store at Sixth and Spruce Streets, equipping it with $3000 worth of fixtures and stock entirely on credit. One of his cherished possessions was a Lippincott soda fountain of Tennessee marble, as ornate as anything of its time. After some tough early years because of a depression following the Fisk-Gould financial crash, the former farm boy's business acumen began to pay off. It was on a brief vacation with his bride at a Jersey farm boarding house that their hostess offered them a temperance drink that really hit the spot. Young Hires thought it the finest home-made herb tea he had ever tasted, and his alert mind immediately sensed its commercial possibilities. The farm woman cheerfully gave him her recipe, took him out in the woods and fields to identify the wild plants whose roots and berries she used — some sixteen in all. These included juniper berries, pipsisewa, spikenard, wintergreen, sarsaparilla and hops, plus caramel.

That capped the climax. "This," reasoned Hires, "is an awful lot of work for a busy housekeeper. Why shouldn't I do the collecting, make packaged extracts of the ingredients, and enable women to prepare this beverage with a fraction of the labor?"

A great deal of experimental work and consultation with medical men and chemists preceded the realization of the dream. When Hires finally offered a sample of his new herb tea for an honest opinion from his friend, the famous Dr. Russell Conwell of "Acres of Diamonds" fame, he got a shrewd reaction.

"This is the best I've ever tasted," pronounced the subsequent patron of Temple University, "but for Heaven's sake don't call it herb tea. Our hard-drinking Pennsylvania coal miners will never touch it under that name. Call it Root Beer."

Thus it was that Hires Root Beer Extract was exhibited at the Philadelphia Centennial in 1876, with samples of the finished product served free.

Featured originally as a temperance drink, and often promoted as a tonic to "purify the blood and make rosy cheeks," it seems odd that Hires should presently run afoul of the W.C.T.U. From about 1895 to 1898, the Women's Christian Temperance Union waged a bitter battle against it in the public press, contending that the fermentation of a sweet liquid in ordinary temperatures always produces alcohol.

But Charles Hires fought back vigorously, albeit in the gentlemanly manner of the Quaker convert he had come to be. His most telling blow was to engage an eminent analytical chemist to analyze the product. The impartial tests demonstrated that the actual alcoholic content of a bottle of Hires Root Beer was less than half that of a homemade loaf of bread. After this opposition gradually disappeared.

WALL PLAQUES

Top row, left to right: Metal lithograph, Lemp Brewery, 1910, 21" diameter; metal lithograph, "Lady Lemp," 1907, 16" diameter; metal lithograph, Lemp Brewery, 1916-1918, 21" diameter.

Center: Sir John Falstaff, Lemp Brewery, has imitation wood-grained frame as part of metal lithograph, about 1914.

Bottom row: Metal lithograph, Lemp Brewery, 1912, 21" diameter; Companion piece to "Lady Lemp" above, Lemp Brewery, 1907; Metal lithograph, "The Home of Falstaff," about 1913, 21" diameter.

CAMPBELL KID POSTERS 8" x 10"

CAMPBELL SOUP COMPANY

The year 1969 marked the beginning of the second century for the Campbell Soup Company. It has been best known for 72 of those years for its line of condensed soups.

What is now one of the world's largest producers of quality convenience foods began in Camden, New Jersey, in 1869. Abram Anderson and Joseph Campbell established a canning and preserving plant that rapidly gained a reputation for its products — preserves, vegetables, salad dressings, and ketchup.

In 1897 a new concept in soups was developed and introduced, a concentrated or condensed soup made by reducing the usual water content, which the homemaker replaced when she prepared the soup. Bulk that made soups expensive at that time was thereby reduced. Because of economies in cans, labels, cartons, shipping weight, and storage space, the development made canned soups something that the average family could afford to buy regularly.

A new red-and-white label made its appearance on Campbell cans in 1898, and legend has it that the color combination was suggested by the school colors of Cornell University. One year later Campbell made its first major advertising expenditure for car cards in New York City streetcars.

The golden medallion, which still decorates the Campbell Soup can today, was awarded to the Company at the Paris International Exposition of 1900 in recognition of the quality of Campbell products.

Magazine advertising began in 1905, and by 1910 there were ads for 21 different soups.

The company maintains a research laboratory devoted entirely to the study of can-making machinery and materials, enamels, closure methods, and evaluation of the finished can itself.

During the 1920s, Franco-American spaghetti products were added to the Campbell line, and in 1929 the Chicago plant began canned foods operations.

At the turn of the century, Grace Gebbie Drayton, a Philadelphia artist, created the now-famous Campbell Kids, launching them in 1904 on a "career" that has made them the most widely featured and lovable characters in the history of advertising.

Mrs. Drayton died in 1936, but the Kids she created have romped through more than a half century in an enormous variety of roles. They rode early-model automobiles and airplanes. They were Liberty Bond salesmen in World War I and air-raid wardens in World War II. They danced the Charleston in the

1920s and were coming out of frozen igloos in the 1950s. In their more recent roles, they take an active part in instructing other youngsters in good manners, good nutrition, and good homemaking.

There have been other artists and studios who have worked on Campbell Kids. They include Grace Weiderseim, Roy Williams, Corrine Pauli, Dorothy Jones, Studio of Paul Fennell, Studio of Johnstone & Cushing, and the Studio of Mel Richman.

Campbell Kids have been used in other ways than in magazine and car card advertising. Various types of dolls have been made down through the years, all of which are avidly sought after by collectors today. As far as it is known, the first dolls were made by the American Doll and Toy Manufacturing Company, which was eventually purchased by the E. I. Horsman Company of New York City. Dolls produced by Horsman were marked " ©1910" and "E. I. H. © 1910." In 1929, the Campbell Soup Company licensed the American Character Doll Company to make another line of Campbell Kid Dolls, and since that time, several dolls have been made by different manufacturers to be used in different promotions.

The use of the Campbell Kids frequently has been accompanied by a jingle. One of the most famous written by Charles M. Synder goes as follows:

"We blend the best with careful pains
in skillful combination.
And every single can contains
our business reputation."

MODERN POSTER
24" x 36"

Famed Pabst gray percherons, first brewery horse team of six to become Grand National Champions. The six-horse hitch won in 1904 at the International Livestock Exposition. The Pabst teams were repeat Grand National winners for many years. Litho prints of the famous six-horse hitch and case-beer wagon were distributed by the thousands.

The Holbert Horse Importing Company was established in 1878 by A. B. Holbert. The firm grew to be the largest of its kind in the United States. This early lithograph measures 28 x 24 inches.

Early tin sign advertises Ebbert farm wagons. Circa 1908.

COURTESY MR. AND MRS. HUGH PARKER
BRITISH HOLLOW ANTIQUES

WELLS FARGO EXPRESS HAULING DR. PEPPER FROM THE PLANT IN WACO, TEXAS

DR PEPPER

Dr Pepper, native "Texan," has one of the most colorful backgrounds of any soft drink on the American market. It begins with a young man who worked at a drug store fountain in Virginia. The owner of the store, a doctor by the name of Pepper, had an attractive daughter who caught the eye of the young man and soon a romance developed between the two.

The doctor, having high aspirations for his daughter, discharged the young man — hoping it would remove him from the scene. It did, temporarily. Heeding the advice of Horace Greeley to "Go West," he traveled to Waco, Texas, where he landed a job at the Old Corner Drug Store.

The romance was not to be thwarted, however. Later the young fountaineer returned to Virginia where he reportedly was successful in his pursuit of the doctor's daughter.

On his trip to Texas, he carried with him his penchant for "discovering" new fountain flavor combinations. One day he hit upon one he liked. Others expressed approval and, having learned of the romance in Virginia, dubbed the new drink Dr Pepper.

R. S. Lazenby, Waco beverage chemist and a patron of the Old Corner Drug Store fountain, became interested and began extensive research on the new drink. In 1885 after some two years of testing, blending and processing, the wonderful new flavor known today as Dr Pepper, was originated and the drink was put on sale commercially. So perfect was his work that the formula has remained basically unchanged.

Little did Lazenby realize at the time that Dr Pepper would become one of the nation's leading

FRAMED SIGN

LITHO PRINT, DATED 1881

soft drinks. Sales and distribution in the beginning were limited to soda fountains in and around Waco, Then Lazenby began bottling Dr Pepper in his Artesian Bottling Works, which made it possible for Dr Pepper to spread its fame and popularity even more rapidly. As early as 1910 Dr Pepper syrup had become one of the principal freight items hauled from Waco by Wells Fargo Express.

It wasn't until 1922, however, when Lazenby's young son-in-law, J. B. O'Hara, came into the business, that Dr Pepper began an extensive sales and distribution program. O'Hara, a young army officer from Pennsylvania, saw great possibilities in Dr Pepper.

In 1922 the company moved to Dallas, Texas. By 1928 the business had grown to such proportions that it was necessary to build new and larger quarters. A modern three-story syrup plant was built in Birmingham, Alabama

A question frequently asked about Dr Pepper is, "What does the 10, 2 and 4 mean?" A Columbia University professor, Dr. Walter H. Eddy, conducting research into the human diet, discovered that three meals per day were insufficient to provide enough energy to keep an active person at top level efficiency. He pinpointed three in-between-meal times during the day when energy in the human body dropped to its lowest ebb. These were 10:30 in the morning, 2:30 and 4:30 in the afternoon.

In a book titled "The Liquid Bite," Dr. Eddy recommended that people avoid these three "let-down" periods and restore energy quickly through food consumed in liquid form, such as in a pure, healthful, soft drink like Dr Pepper. Thus Dr. Pepper incorporated the times 10, 2 and 4 o'clock into its trademark as a reminder that Dr Pepper consumed at these hours provides a lift to offset these low energy periods.

In the main lobby of Dr Pepper Company in Dallas are four colorful murals depicting the origin of carbonated beverages. Natural carbonated water has been known to man through the ages and has intrigued the imagination. Its origin dates back to the ancient Greeks who were among the first to enjoy the "sparkling water" which bubbled from natural springs.

In the 17th century a Belgian chemist, J. B. Van Helmont, first recognized carbon dioxide as the "wild spirit" of the mineral water. To Dr. Joseph Priestley, English scientist, goes the credit for inventing artificially carbonated water.

After 1772, there was a rapidly increasing appreciation of artificially carbonated waters and some progress was made in their manufacture on a commercial scale.

EARLY AND DARING POSTER
CIRCA 1900

RELEASED JULY 30, 1932

The ranks of collectors of Disney posters and theater displays is increasing rapidly each year. These displays of Walt Disney's first animated characters, Mickey and Minnie Mouse, date back to the early 1930s and are particularly collectible. The Silly Symphony — Flower and Trees poster, above, was the first picture released of the now famous Silly Symphony series.

early theater lobby displays

Old handbills, broadside, movie and circus posters are becoming more and more collectible. Many of the early posters and lobby displays had vividly colored lithographed scenes promoting the circus, carnival, singers, dancers, magic acts, mind reading, and road shows. The old Laurel and Hardy posters enjoy a new popularity today, as do all of Walt Disney's animated characters.

Also, there is a growing interest among collectors for the old glass projection slides. These double glass slides were used by movie houses to advertise products — or coming attractions — during the silent film days.

SEPTEMBER 17, 1932

EARLY METAL SIGN CIRCA 1898

OVAL METAL PLAQUE
CIRCA 1900

METAL PLAQUE OR TRAY
CIRCA 1900

86

EARLY LITHOGRAPH, CIRCA 1880

U.S. BORAX & CHEMICAL CORPORATION

Shortly before the Civil War, borax crystals were discovered in certain mineral springs and lakes north of San Francisco. However, it wasn't until eight years after the discovery, that the Borax Company could raise sufficient capital to start operations at one of the lake sites.

In 1870 "cottonball" was found in quantity on the Nevada Desert and the borax industry began. Cottonball was ulexite, one of the borate minerals, which lay in shimmering masses on the ancient, arid lake bed of Columbus Marsh, Nevada.

F. M. "Borax" Smith, was one of the first great names in the new industry, founding the Pacific Coast Borax Company. He was a Michigan farm boy who had come West in an unsuccessful search for gold. When the word of the cottonball strikes reached him in 1872, he headed for the Nevada desert, hoping to sell firewood to borax manufacturers who needed fuel to process the ore. Once there, Smith quickly recognized the great potentialities of borax itself, and staked out claims. One by one he bought out his competitors, becoming a powerful figure in the new industry.

The distributing agency for Smith's borax was William T. Coleman & Company of San Francisco. With a growing demand for borax and an apparently unlimited reserve of crude ore, Coleman had to find the quickest, surest way to move his product out of Death Valley, across 165 barren miles of desert to the nearest railroad junction at Majave.

Wagons pulled by multiple mule teams were not unknown in the desert in those days, but it was J. W. S. Perry, Coleman's superintendent, and a young muleskinner named Ed Stiles, who thought of the idea of hitching two ten-mule teams together to form a hundred-foot long twenty-mule team. Perry designed wagons massive and sturdy enough to carry the borax and withstand the rugged journey, while Perry laid out the most suitable route for the mule teams.

The wagons, which were built in Majave for $900, had rear wheels seven feet high and front wheels five feet high, each with steel tires eight inches wide and one inch thick. The hubs were 18 inches in diameter and 22 inches in length. The spokes, of split oak, measured 5½ inches wide at the hub, and the axle-trees were made of solid steel bars, 3½ inches square. The wagon beds were 16 feet long, 4 feet wide and 6 feet deep. Empty, each wagon weighed 7,800 pounds, and when loaded with borax it weighed 31,800 pounds.

From 1883 to 1889, the twenty-mule teams hauled borax out of Death Valley, over the steep Panamint Mountains and across the desert to the railroad. Despite the heat — and temperatures often rose to 130 degrees — the teams pulled their heavy loads, traveling fifteen to eighteen miles a day.

The twenty-mule teams soon became a world famous symbol, the trademark first of the Pacific Coast Borax Company, and today of the many products made by U.S. Borax.

It should be noted here that one of the first advertising booklets recommended the use of borax for digestion; to keep milk sweet; as a complexion aid ("Don't wash your face in ordinary lake water"); to remove dandruff; and for the bath. Borax was also "excellent for washing carriages" and useful in curing epilepsy and bunions. The present company, of course, does not advertise borax for such uses. Today, much of the world's industry depends on borates. Boric acid, borax and other compounds of boron are used in almost every major industry, and are essential to modern agriculture.

ADVERTISING MIRRORS

Mirrors became a popular form of advertising during the early years of this century. They were generally celluloid backed and designed to attract the feminine members of the family. However, there were mirrors with masculine appeal. These were issued by fraternal organizations, tobacco companies, insurance companies, and brewers.

The most popular design of all is the mirror which illustrates birthstones on the backside. These were made by the Cruver Manufacturing Company for jewelers and the Parisian Novelty Company for the manufacturers. Even political campaign mirrors carried birthstone designs.

Most advertising mirrors were circular two inches in diameter, while others were rectangular or oval. The larger ones were weighted and used as paperweights.

EARLY ADVERTISING POSTER
DATED 1905

Favored
—for
50 Years

CARDBOARD SIGN

QUAKER OATS COMPANY

Ferdinand Schumacher, a German immigrant, introduced stoneground oatmeal into the North American diet, beginning a revolution in breakfast food, which led to a business that made him Akron's Oatmeal King.

By the time the Quaker Oats Company was founded at the turn of the century oatmeal was a big business.

The Quaker symbol was given commercial form in 1877 when the Quaker Mill Company registered as a trademark the figure of a man in Quaker garb, to which in 1895 the word "Quaker" was added in another registry. The 1877 filing was America's first registered trademark for a breakfast cereal.

Quaker was a pioneer in mass-media advertising and effective promotion campaigns, which made it a giant in the business. First of millions of Quaker comic books (16-page grasshopper circus) were distributed as early as 1894. Early-day advertising men also literally brought Aunt Jemima to life.

WORLD'S FAIR BEER

Wm. J. LEMP Brewing Co.
ST. LOUIS, MO. U.S.A.

TIN SIGN

FIRST REGISTERED TRADEMARK FOR A CEREAL

DARING ADVERTISEMENT FROM McCLURE'S MAGAZINE, 1897

CARLING'S 1840 NINE PINTS OF THE LAW
BY LAWSON WOOD

COURTESY WANDA SANDERS

METAL SIGN

COURTESY KEN BASSETT

CARDBOARD SIGN

Old lithograph, used to promote Schlitz beer around the turn of the century. The girl pictured is a variation of the "Schlitz Purity Girl," adopted in the 1880s.

Statue to the right, with a "globe" body (company trademark), was made in various sizes during the late nineteenth century.

GRANITE HANGING SIGN
COURTESY STANDARD BRANDS, INC.

STANDARD BRANDS

When Standard Brands was formed in 1929, there were brought into the organization three highly successful companies, The Fleischmann Company, Royal Baking Powder Company, and Chase & Sanborn. All had grown from small beginnings to national prominence in the food market. The story of three companies and how they came to be united into one great company forms an absorbing romance of modern American business.

CHASE AND SANBORN

Chase and Sanborn is another Civil War child. It was formed in 1863 by two Boston merchants, Caleb Chase and James S. Sanborn.

This old firm of coffee and tea merchants was always a leader in its field. In 1878, it was the first to pack roasted coffee in sealed cans. Expanding business made necessary the opening of a new plant and offices in Chicago in 1880. Two years later a Canadian branch was established at Montreal. At the Chicago World's Fair in 1893 Chase & Sanborn's Seal Brand Coffee was served exclusively.

THE FLEISCHMANN COMPANY

In the early 1860s Charles Fleischmann, was the "still master" on a great estate in Hungary. He brewed all the spirits used by the people living on the estate, and also made yeast. About 1865 Charles came to America to attend the wedding of his sister. He was surprised at the poor quality of the bread here, and as an expert on yeast he determined that the cause of this was the uncertain and generally poor quality of the yeast which was homemade by the bakers themselves. After the wedding, Charles went back to Hungary with a budding idea. As time went on, he foresaw more and more clearly the big future awaiting the men who would make possible the baking of bread in America as good as that produced by the bakers in his native land. A few years after his first visit, Charles Fleischmann returned here to carry out his plan of supplying this country with better bread.

With his brother Maximilian, he joined forces with James M. Gaff of Cincinnati to form Gaff, Fleischmann & Company, and in 1868 began the manufacture of the first compressed yeast in the United States. The first yeast was sold from a basket by Charles Fleischmann himself. Later he secured a horse and wagon. In 1879 Gaff died, and shortly thereafter the firm was renamed Fleischmann & Company.

The progress of the new firm was slow but steady. It was no small task to educate bakers to the use of compressed yeast, for old habits were hard to change. In a few years Fleischmann's Yeast had obtained considerable local distribution. It was not until 1876, when the firm put all its resources into a Model Vienna Bakery at the Centennial Exposition in Philadelphia, that its fame began to spread to all parts of the United States. Bread and rolls made with compressed yeast were labeled and served where everyone could see the process. Commercial bakers and home-baking women from all sections of the country saw the excellent results. The demand became so great that a plant was established on Long Island, and plans were laid for a large plant at Peekskill, N.Y.

Following the Centennial Exposition, Fleischmann & Company entered a new era of growth. Gradually, compressed yeast supplanted other forms of yeast in the commercial industry, and a large homebaking market using the yeast was built up.

The firm was incorporated in 1905 as The Fleischmann Company.

*Today these advertisements from 1920 magazines,
framed and ready for hanging, are being offered for
sale in antique shops and collectors' shows.*

ORIGINAL POSTER OF THE UNEEDA BISCUIT BOY
COURTESY MRS. JOHN SCHOONMAKER

EARLY POSTER

NATIONAL BISCUIT COMPANY

It was Adolphus W. Green who finally took the cracker out of the barrel — undermining the symbol and exposing it as an unsanitary hangover from frontier days. Green, one of the founders of the National Biscuit Company, put his revolutionary ideas into action by embarking on a packaging and promotional upheaval — the creation of brand names that opened the way for modern supermarkets.

The National Biscuit Company has been a leader in the nation's cookie and cracker business since its formation in 1898. Prior to Nabisco's founding, operations within the industry were largely local in nature and product quality ranged from very good to very poor. Packaging and distribution were major problems. The cracker barrel, with its many deficiencies, was the hallmark of every grocery store.

Back at the turn of the century, National Biscuit Company took its first important step toward creating its "coat of arms." NABISCO used a symbol that had an ancient origin. In prehistoric times, the circle and the cross with two bars were used to represent the creation of life. In the early Christian era, this same symbol stood for the triumph of spiritual over worldly things.

During the 15th century, this symbol was used as a printer's mark by the Society of Printers in Venice. And in 1900 A. W. Green, then chairman of the board of National Biscuit Company, familiar with the history of this symbol, suggested that it be incorporated in a "coat of arms" for the company. The "coat of arms" went through a number of changes from 1900 through the years, but the basic design and symbol stayed much the same.

THE ROYAL BAKING POWDER COMPANY

The Royal Baking Powder Company began its career in a small way out in Indiana. Women had been accustomed to buying baking soda and cream of tartar for cakes and biscuits. During the Civil War period a drugstore in Fort Wayne, Indiana, began to combine the two and sell them as "baking powder." The new product met with an immediate favorable response. By 1875 the Royal Baking Powder Company had grown to such an extent that its plant and offices were moved to Chicago. In 1899 the main offices were transferred to New York and the company continued a steady growth. A few years before the formation of Standard Brands, Royal Gelatin Desserts were added to the Royal line.

Tins and Containers

Nicholas Appert, a Frenchman, is generally credited with the discovery of food preservation by canning, and it is believed but not fully documented that one William Underwood started the first American canning operation in Boston in 1819, using Appert's procedure. And by 1820 Underwood (in Boston) and Thomas Kensett (in New York) were both in commercial production of canned foods.

The first sanitary can was introduced commercially about 1900, and basically, this is the tin can we know today.

The discovery of tinplating is said to have been made by an English tin miner in Bohemia during the 13th century. The name "tin can" is derived from the English designation "tin cannister."

Early cans were made by hand. The process was laborious, and even the more expert artisans could turn out no more than a few cans a day. These were of heavy gauge tin-plate. Because there was no classic pattern that should be followed, these craftsmen used their imagination freely, usually creating many quaint and intriguing designs. The exquisitely decorated Huntley and Palmer's biscuit tins are excellent examples. They were among the earliest tins used to package a product, and naturally the cans are eagerly sought by collectors today.

During the mid-19th century, Somers Brothers of Brooklyn, New York, devised a technique of applying a lithographed design directly to the metal instead of upon a paper wrapper. But it wasn't until the last quarter of the 19th century, that the small container became a necessity.

In the early days of the country store, very little attention was given to the identification of brands, simply because most staples, including tobacco, tea, sugar, coffee, etc., were sold in bulk form from large bins. But as business developed during the 1870s and 1880s, so did competition, especially among the large tobacco companies. They quickly saw that if they were to attract the customer, they would have to remove their tobacco from the big, drab bins, and package it attractively enough to stimulate sales. Thus began the manufacture of

the imaginative and colorful tobacco containers. To prolong the life of these advertising tins, it became important to give the container a secondary use — thus small canisters were made which were used as bins for flour, sugar, spices, etc. in the kitchen. "Lunchbox" tins were made with handles, so they could be used to carry lunch to school, or for use as a general utilitarian tin box in the home. The small pocket tins were handy for storing nails, screws, etc., after the tobacco had been smoked up or chewed. But during the 1920s, the effort to out-do the competitors' package declined, and eventually led to the undecorative cardboard, tin, and plastic containers made today.

Can collections have developed rapidly during the last few years, and very liberal offers are frequently made for especially wanted items, notably a Mayo's Humpty-Dumpty type tin, or an imaginative English biscuit tin created in the shape of a book by Huntley & Palmers of England. Such examples are now accepted as package collector's classics. In this particular field, strangely enough, it is the shape rather than age that is the criterion of value and desirability.

Tin containers were made in countless shapes, sizes, and colors, for almost every type of product, including tobacco, foodstuffs, gun powder, chemicals, medicines, soaps, and a wide diversity of other non-food products. Some bore paper labels; on others the name of the manufacturer and product were painted on, stamped into metal, or embossed.

Many companies which manufactured the early tins are no longer in existence. However, there are those that have survived to become well-known brands on the grocery shelves today. Containers bearing the latter brand names are of greater value, fetching record prices when sold.

Although the tin container enjoys the greatest popularity in this field, others too are collectible, such as the container made of glass, pottery, wood, paper, or cardboard. These novelties range from root beer mugs, the fancy Teaberry gum stands, Planters Peanut jars, Maxwell House coffee cups,

BLUE BOAR TOBACCO TIN
STAMP DATED 1910

and ceramic wall plaques. Many of these items are of great interest to business firms which assemble museum material relating to the history of their product, and to collectors of restoration villages and old-time country stores.

There is also a demand for early boxes and crates by the country store enthusiasts. Some remove the ends of these cases which are covered with paper labels, and hang them as a picture. These too are entertaining bits of advertising Americana.

Few tin containers manufactured today in quantity are exciting enough from a collector's point of view to rival the fine early examples, and happily, there is little indication that duplicates of the early containers will ever be re-introduced. Hence, the value of interesting tin collections will not suffer from excessive duplication as other objects have — but will continue to increase in value with each passing year.

EARLY TOBACCO TIN

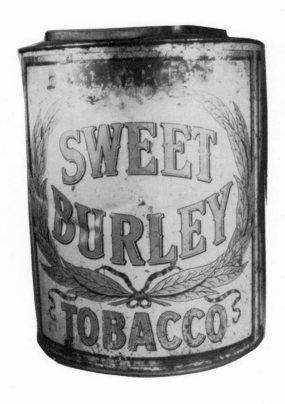

WOODEN CIGAR BOX
DATED 1893
4½" WIDE, 13½" LONG

PRINCE ALBERT TINS DATE   BACK TO 1909

CIGARETTE TIN

DATED 1917

FIVE-POUND TOBACCO TIN
8½" x 10", 8" HIGH

DATED 1922

CAMEL CIGARS

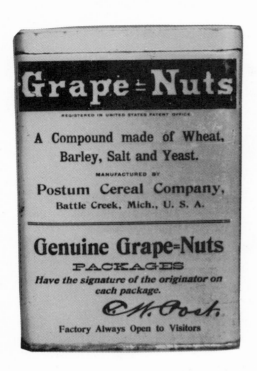

GENERAL FOODS

Food is America's biggest business, and General Foods is a part of that business. The packaged grocery industry is a product of modern America. A few branded, packaged groceries were sold during the 19th century, but it wasn't until the turn of the century that the packaged grocery business really began to take hold.

In this century, packaged groceries have played an increasingly important part in bringing food from America's farms and other world sources to consumers' tables. They ended the cracker barrel era when most food was offered to the consumer in bulk.

General Foods' well-known brands include Maxwell House Coffee, Jell-O, Bird's Eye, Post, Baker's, and Kool-Aid. Other brands are Sanka, Yuban, Minute, D-Zerta, Swans Down, Good Seasons, Log Cabin, Calumet, Gaines, LaFrance, Certo, S.O.S., and in Britain, Bird's.

Most of General Food's present-day operating divisions were pioneering as independent companies long before 1925. It was in that year that the Postum Cereal Company, Inc., entered into the first of a series of consolidations resulting in the organization which in 1929 took the name of General Foods.

The Jell-O Company was the first to join the Postum organization in 1925. Then came Igleheart Brothers and Minute Tapioca in 1926. Log Cabin syrup joined in 1927, Calumet Baking Powder, Maxwell House and La France in 1928, and Certo a year later.

The beginnings of Maxwell House Coffee go back to the 1890s, Swans Down Cake Flour to 1876, Jell-O and Franklin Baker Coconut to 1897, Post Toasties to 1904 (originally called Elijah's Manna), Calumet Baking Powder to 1889, and Log Cabin Syrup to 1887.

Log Cabin syrup tins have been especially popular among collectors. P. J. Towle first manufactured the syrup in 1887 at St. Paul, Minnesota. Towle introduced his syrup in house shaped tins. His log cabin tin wasn't used until the present century. General Foods distributed the syrup in log cabin tins from 1927 until World War II when the syrup was packaged in glass bottles.

TOWLE'S LOG CABIN SYRUP TIN

Note on bottom of can reads: "From my cabin to your table," and signed Jack Towle.

COURTESY MRS. CHARLES FREEMAN

HUNTLEY & PALMERS

For more than a century the name Huntley & Palmers has been familiar to the people of Reading, England. In 1826, Reading was a small but prosperous market for the produce of Berkshire Farms. This produce provided Thomas Huntley, a local baker, with the ingredients for making appetizing biscuits and cakes. Some of these were sold locally and others were supplied to the weary and hungry travelers on the stage coach which stopped opposite his shop on the main highway between London and Bath. In this way the quality of his goods became known far beyond Reading. The original shop in London Street still exists.

Actually, the Huntley and Palmers story really begins with Mrs. Hannah Huntley, the wife of a Quaker schoolmaster who lived at the top of Burford Hill.

Coaches stopped outside the Huntley cottage to give the horses a rest after slogging up the slope. Mrs. Huntley started selling her delicious flat cakes to the travellers. She was so successful that in 1822 she and her son Thomas started up a business in Reading's London Street.

The little bakery and shop soon became a thriving business, spreading the fame of Thomas Huntley's biscuits all over the South of England.

Coaches from London to the West Country regularly stopped at the Crown Hotel right opposite the shop and Thomas would send someone over to sell biscuits to the passengers.

In 1841 the Bath to London stagecoach brought George Palmer, another Quaker, to visit Thomas Huntley, who was his cousin by marriage. Thomas and George went into partnership — and Huntley and Palmers was born.

There remained the problem of keeping high quality biscuits fresh on their way to other parts of the country or overseas. By a happy coincidence, Thomas Huntley's brother, Joseph, had an ironmonger's shop in London Street, opposite the bakery. Here, he started making airtight tin boxes in which biscuits stayed crisp for much longer than previously. This small shop has since become Huntley, Boorne & Stevens, of which the present Lord Palmer is chairman.

George Palmer's brothers, Samuel and William

105

BISCUIT TIN REPRESENTS BOOK CASE
FILLED WITH BOOKS

Isaac, joined the firm and when Thomas Huntley died in 1857, the three of them went into partnership on their own. Six of their descendants still serve on the Huntley and Palmers board.

By the mid 1860s the Palmer brothers were selling biscuits in China, the United States, West Africa, Brazil, Portugal, Spain, Turkey, Scandinavia and Russia. And they were also supplying Queen Victoria.

When George Palmer died in 1897, the biscuit company employed more than 7,000 people.

The designers of Huntley and Palmers biscuit tins had vivid imaginations, creating many unusual shapes and designs. Many of their decorative and reusable tin boxes resemble sets of books, fishing hampers, clocks, log cabins, old stage coach lights, and even roulette wheels. Naturally, all of these are eagerly sought by collectors today. And happily for the collector, Huntley and Palmers' products are still being made and sold in attractive lithographed gift tins, with many designs inspired by Josiah Wedgwood & Sons Limited.

WATKINS PRODUCTS, INC.

One man . . . one product . . . one idea. This was the very inconspicuous start of what is today Watkins Products, Inc., one of the largest direct selling firms in the world.

The man was Joseph R. Watkins. The product was liniment. The idea was simple — to bring the product to the customer's door.

Watkins, a native of Ohio, came to the Midwest with his family in 1862. His father, the Rev. B. U. Watkins, chose to settle in Plainview, Minnesota, a small town in the southeastern part of the state. Plainview was destined to be the birthplace of a world-wide business.

The eventful day was in 1868, when Watkins was 28 years old. He purchased, from Dr. Richard Ward of Cincinnati, Ohio, the rights to manufacture and sell a liniment and various other medicinal products the doctor had been using in his practice. Watkins produced the merchandise, bottled it, and with horse and buggy toured the local villages and farms.

In 1885 a transformation took place that eventually led to the world-wide distribution of Watkins products. It was that year that Watkins moved his business to Winona, Minnesota, where it is presently located.

During the late 1880s, Watkins began to visualize the potential for his type of business. Demand was spreading as dealers, in the horse and wagon tradition, picked up the Watkins idea as well as the products and carried them to all parts of the Midwest. About 1893, a South Dakota dealer named York enjoyed successful selling, so Watkins arranged for him to go to San Francisco, and there established the first Watkins branch office.

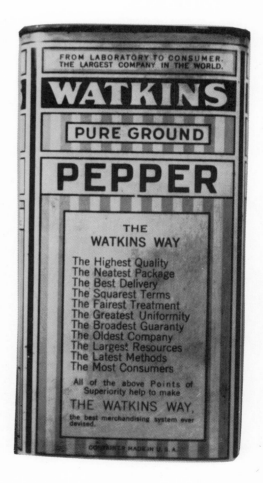

By this time the Watkins line was beginning to take shape, and the products included the original Liniment, Improved Condition Powder, Egyptian Stick Salve, Vegetable Cathartic Pills, and Peptro-Carbo Salve. The product labels carried reproductions of Watkins' visage and signature.

During the first decade of this century, the pulse of the business steadily quickened. Branch offices sprang up in Tennessee and Maryland. Exploitation of international markets began in 1915. A branch was established in Australia, and within ten years similar arrangements were made in Africa and New Zealand.

Today, with 100 years in its wake and a fifth president at the helm, James N. Doyle, Watkins stands on the threshold of a new century.

THE KELLOGG COMPANY

In the year 1874 a sleigh or buggy was the means of transportation for a boy of fourteen who sold brooms made in his father's factory. Today, high speed trucks and trains quickly carry the millions of cases of ready-to-eat cereals from the huge, modern manufacturing plant built by the man who started his career so modestly. This is the story of Will Keigh Kellogg, who was responsible to a large degree, for changing the eating habits of the American people through the development and production of crisp, wholesome, and appetizing cereals.

Like most new ideas, the suggestion of ready-to-eat cereals was ridiculed. "Make a palatable food from corn? Impossible! No one will eat the stuff!" These were the comments of Mr. Kellog's friends when he established a factory for manufacture of Corn Flakes in 1906. But his friends were wrong, because the public liked Corn Flakes, and the demand for the product was so great that within one year the daily production of 4,000 cases was insufficient.

The first Kellogg Corn Flakes were manufactured in a small wooden building which burned to the ground just about a year after Mr. Kellogg had started production. Mr. Kellogg immediately began construction of a modern factory which would provide for expanded production. Today, the building complex at the Battle Creek facility contains 47 acres of floor space, where 4,400 employees prepare, package, and ship 9,000,000 to 10,000,000 packages of ready-to-eat cereal daily.

Many people ask, "Why did W. K. Kellogg locate in Battle Creek?" The Battle Creek Sanitarium was established in Battle Creek, Michigan, about 1875, with Dr. John Harvey Kellogg heading the group, with his brother W. K. Kellogg as business manager. As part of their work in trying to improve the food so that is might be digested more easily, the Kellogg brothers experimented with grains. As a result of these experiments, they discovered how to make flaked cereals such as corn flakes, wheat, and rice. Since the Sanitarium was located in Battle Creek, and many of the patients of the Sanitarium were interested in the "health foods" such as corn flakes, it seemed only a natural location for the plant.

From this humble beginning in 1906, the company has grown to an international organization which has made Corn Flakes known to practically every nation of the free world.

CLABBER GIRL
BAKING POWDER

Based in Terre Haute, Indiana, the Hulman Company was organized in 1850. Its business at that time was first retail, and then wholesale grocery and general merchandise. In 1899, Clabber Girl Baking Powder was copyrighted. It was first manufactured and sold only in Indiana and Illinois. In 1929, the company began to expand to national distribution and this was accomplished by 1933. The early advertising signs which introduced Clabber Girl Baking Powder to the housewives of America were distributed during the period between 1929 through 1940.

COURTESY HULMAN & COMPANY, TERRE HAUTE

TIN WITH PAPER LABEL
DATED 1899

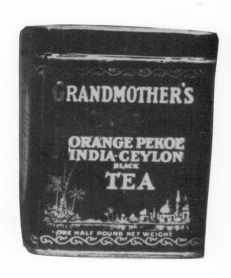

109

EARLY COFFEE TINS COURTESY PAUL AND UILA HARMAN

LIBBY, McNEILL & LIBBY

Chicago and the canning industry were relative infants when two young brothers, Arthur A. And Charles P. Libby, migrated to the city during the troubled years immediately preceding the American Civil War.

At age 26 Arthur A. Libby came west from Portland, Maine, in 1857. His younger brother came to Chicago the following year. Both secured employment with an uncle, John C. Hancock, at the meat packing firm of Cragin & Company.

Official records indicate that the firm of A. A. Libby and Company began packing products in April 1868.

It is also known that Charles P. Libby and Archibald McNeill joined the founder in the young firm in 1868. Pooling meagre resources and tireless devotion, they founded a business which is today worldwide in scope and unsurpassed in its reputation for producing quality food products.

Arthur A. Libby was unquestionably the moving force during those early years. Friends reported years later how he would rise before dawn and personally select cattle from the cattle markets to be driven to his plant. He saw a future in canned meats and began experimenting with tapered tin for improved hand packing in 1872. In 1875, he secured patent rights to a successful tapered tin which allowed packing of superior compressed corned beef. One year later he and his partners exported their first canned corned beef to Britain, and the firm was on its way to international prominence.

By the mid-1880s, the firm was recognized as the world's largest packer of canned meats. Success came dear to these enterprising young men. Archibald McNeill retired due to ill health in 1888 at the age of 52. Arthur A. Libby also retired in ill health in 1890. Charles P. Libby became president of the company and continued in that position until his death at the age of 57 in 1895.

Collectors of Libby's early advertising material will be interested in knowing that in 1877 Libby advertised canned corned beef on colorful picture postcards. The first advertising calendars were distributed at the Columbian Exposition in Chicago in 1893. They show beef extract, beef tongues, boiled beef, roast beef, lunch tongues, roast mutton, boiled mutton, deviled ham, chipped beef, potted ham, potted tongue and turkey and tongue soups. In 1900 colorful Libby's souvenir bookmarks were distributed at the Universal Exposition in Paris, and at the Pan-American Exposition in Buffalo, N.Y. the following year.

COURTESY MR. AND MRS. J. C. DILLINGHAM

1925 LIBBY TIN

STORY OF JOHNSON WAX

Among the English colonists who settled in the Connecticut Valley in 1626 was Henry Johnson. His descendants lived on the same farm for the next 180 years until Phineas Johnson and his wife left to head west in a Conestoga wagon. At Elyria, Ohio, December 24, 1833, a son was born, Samuel Curtis Johnson. This son was destined fifty-three years later to found a small company that was to become the world's largest manufacturer of wax products.

Young Johnson's first business training came as office boy with the Milwaukee & LaCrosse Railroad at Milwaukee. In 1861 he married and for a number of years operated a book store and stationery business in Kenosha. In 1882 Johnson went to Racine and joined the Racine Hardware Manufacturing Company as a salesman for parquetry flooring. The home fashions of the period dictated the use of heavily fringed velvet curtains and oriental rugs

113

framed by the geometric patterns of parquetry flooring made up of small blocks of wood of different hues. Four years after he joined the hardware firm, Johnson purchased the flooring business from his employer.

At the age of 53 he founded his own company in 1886. Five days each week he traveled the countryside in his buggy, selling flooring to contractors for fine homes, churches, hotels, and public buildings. On the sixth day he returned to Racine to fill orders and to tend to his responsibilities as manager of the business. In 1892 he took his son, Herbert F. Johnson, Sr., into the firm.

Customers who had purchased Johnson flooring began to write asking for the best way to take care of their new floors.

Mr. Johnson knew that parquet floors had originated in Europe and for centuries had withstood the tramp of thousands of boots. The floors of old castles had been protected and maintained with wax.

He studied waxes — one in particular which comes from the leaves of a Brazilian palm called Carnauba. Using Carnauba and other ingredients, a paste wax formula was developed. Johnson decided to sell it as a sideline to the flooring business. Cans of the prepared paste wax were sent with each new floor, and advertised in periodicals of the day. Steadily the demand for the wax increased.

In 1906, Johnson made his son a partner in the firm, and the company became S. C. Johnson & Son. He died in 1919 at the age of 86, but he lived to see Johnson products receive international acclaim. His son, Herbert F., succeeded him as president.

Since Johnson Wax was established, its history has been marked by enterprise growth, based on the philosophy of the founder — that if you make something better than your competitor and properly tell others about it, people will insist on buying it. Through the years this philosophy has helped to establish the name of Johnson Wax around the world.

COURTESY CRAIG VANIS

THE LIPTON STORY

Thomas Lipton dropped out of school at age 10, and job-hopped around Scotland until he was fired for "an oversight in performing one of his duties." At 14, he left home and headed for America with little money and even less of an idea of what he would do when he got there.

Once in the States, he held no less than ten jobs during the next few years, staying only as long as his interest was held. On one occasion he even stowed away on a cargo ship from North Carolina to New York. After the ship dropped her pilot at Fort Sumter, he presented himself to the captain who allowed him to earn his passage by doing deck work.

Young Thomas finally found himself a job as an assistant in a prosperous grocery store in New York. Here his restless spirit found direction. With all his energies harnessed, he concentrated on learning the up-to-date methods of the store and prepared himself for the career as a merchant that won him worldwide fame.

By the time he was 19 he had received several promotions and had saved $500. Now, he decided, was the time to return to Glasgow and his parents.

Although delighted to have him home again, they weren't enthusiastic about his plans for expanding the family business. When his parents would not let young Lipton risk their hard-earned money to start another shop he used his own savings to buy a number of hams and bacons at an auction of a ship's cargo. He then sold these to small shopkeepers at such a considerable profit that he was able to convince his parents he was worthy of their backing.

On his 21st birthday, Thomas Lipton started business on his own in a small provisions shop. In a few years he owned 20 stores.

Since the success of his shops presented a new problem — sources of supply, he turned his attention toward America again and decided to explore the feasibility of acquiring a stockyard of his own in Chicago. After visiting several, he found what he wanted, a building with the facilities for killing and dressing 400 pigs a day. The packing house was in operation ten days after he first arrived in the city.

It was between the years of 1888 and 1898 that Lipton took an interest in the tea trade. He developed a superior blend of tea, and one of the first innovations was to have his teas packaged in pound, half-pound and quarter-pound packets. The previous general practice in the retail trade was to sell tea from open chests or drawers.

Lipton's packages — plainly marked with price, weight and quality — were instantly popular.

Because of a failure in the Ceylon coffee crop, Lipton was able to buy a number of plantations at a low price and replanted these with tea.

From the beginning he reorganized the tea production methods on his Ceylon estates. Before his time, most of the Ceylon tea had been transported to the valleys by native carriers. Lipton set up a system of aerial wireways between the tea gardens on the hills and the factories at the base. The tea was placed in strong bags, which were sent whizzing down the wires, right to the doors of the factories.

"Direct from the Tea Garden to the Tea Pot!"

Because of his success in Ceylon, he decided to enter the American tea trade. A year and a half after buying his first Ceylon plantations, Lipton was selling more tea in America and Canada than he thought would ever be possible. From this the present company, Thomas J. Lipton, Inc., had its beginnings.

The earliest package in the files of the American branch of Lipton's is the red-label tin of 1910 vintage, with double closure to protect tea from moisture. Lipton's first tea bags were tied and trimmed by hand. By 1927 manufacture was automatic.

A VARIETY OF EARLY ADVERTISING COLLECTIBLES

Advertising Novelties

BOOKLETS

Advertising booklets were popular during the 1880-1900 period. They contained amusing stories, jokes, humorous line drawings, and information of general interest to the public. There were advertiseing booklets for home furnishings; farm and business; service, which includes insurance, railroad, telegraph, etc.; clothing, tobacco, foods, and an array of personal accessories such as perfumes, medicines, jewelry, dyes, threads, etc.

Advertising booklets, such as the one pictured here, were popular during the 1880-1900 period. These small booklets essentially contained amusing stories, jokes, humorous line drawings, information of general interest — with a liberal interlarding of testimonials and advertising claims.

PABST SOUVENIR SPOON
ISSUED 1893

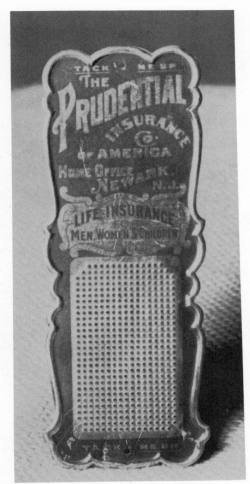

MATCHSCRATCHER — CIRCA 1905

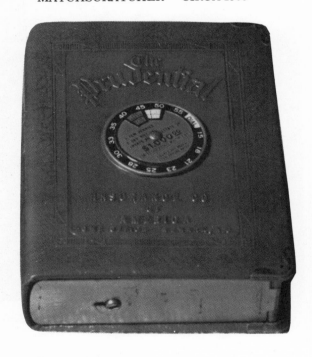

CELLULOID MR. PEANUT SALT AND PEPPER SHAKERS 3¾" HIGH

PLANTERS PEANUT

In 1961, Standard Brands acquired the Planters Nut and Chocolate Company, the nation's leading processor of peanuts. Its principal products are salted peanuts, peanut candy, peanut butter, and peanut oil. Dry roasted peanuts, cashews and mixed nuts are also processed by this division.

The "Planters" history is most interesting, beginning about 1876 near Venice, Italy. In the small town of Oderzo was born a boy who was named Amedeo Obici. When the lad was about twelve years old, he came to America to live with an uncle in Scranton, Pennsylvania. As soon as young Amedeo gained command of simple English, he moved to nearby Wilkes-Barre and increased his earnings with a fruit stand. He studied the English language, mostly at night, reading many books to improve his general education.

Obici never forgot his native Italy, and by the time he neared adulthood he was saving most of the sixty dollars a month he was earning to pay passage to the United States for his mother, sisters, and a brother.

When Obici opened his own fruit stand, he invested in a peanut roaster, became more interested in peanuts, and sought to improve their taste.

A few years later he dubbed himself "The Peanut Specialist" and turned peddler, using a horse and wagon to take his peanuts to other storekeepers. Within a short time he had developed his own method of blanching whole roasted peanuts, doing away with the hulls and skins.

In 1906 at the age of twenty-nine, Obici went into

Also called "match safes," these were distributed by several companies during the 1880s and 1890s. This one, patented August 14, 1883, bears the company name and registered trademark. Note the rough surface on the bottom for striking matches.

COURTESY ANHEUSER-BUSCH, INC.

SKILLET CLOCK
CIRCA 1890

partnership with his future brother-in-law, Mario Peruzzi, a native of his region of Italy. The two young men rented a small factory for twenty-five dollars a month, installed two large roasters and some crude machinery, and employed six people.

"Planters" sounded important and dignified to Obici, and a sign on the front of the building identified the business as Planters Peanut Company.

Dealers were supplied with glass display jars and a cup to measure out the right quantity. A horse and cart was used to distribute the plant's production to stores. Two years later, with Obici still serving as president and general manager, the firm was incorporated as Planters Nut and Chocolate Company and capitalized at $50,000.

As the business grew and prospered, a series of innovations lengthened the company's leadership strides. The year 1916 saw the birth of "Mr. Peanut," and his association with the company's brand name. Seeking an animated symbol, Obici offered a prize for the best sketch. It was a fourteen-year-old Suffolk school boy who submitted the winning drawing, an animated peanut. A commercial artist added the hat, monocle and cane to the peanut figure.

Obici crashed into national advertising in 1916, and immediately the jovial little peanut man began to please the public eye.

BOTH SIDES OF CARDBOARD FAN
EARLY 1900s

MOXIE

One of the oldest names in the soft drink business is "Moxie." It appeared on the market in Boston, Massachusetts, in 1885, during the patent medicine heydey, and has been in continuous production since that time.

George Archer organized the company to make Moxie Nerve Food, but the Pure Food and Drug Law of 1906 forced modification of formulas for practically everyone in the medicine business.

Archer, spurred by the growing soft drink market, plunged into an advertising campaign to publicize his product by introducing a variety of novelties, many of which are still around. His toy Moxie-Mobile is particularly desirable as a collector's item, in addition to cardboard fans, change trays, bottles, serving glasses, and bottle openers.

The company was sold in 1967, and in 1969 it acquired the National Nugrape Company and moved from Boston to Atlanta. During the following year it acquired Monarch Citrus Products of Doraville, Georgia, which is home base for the company today.

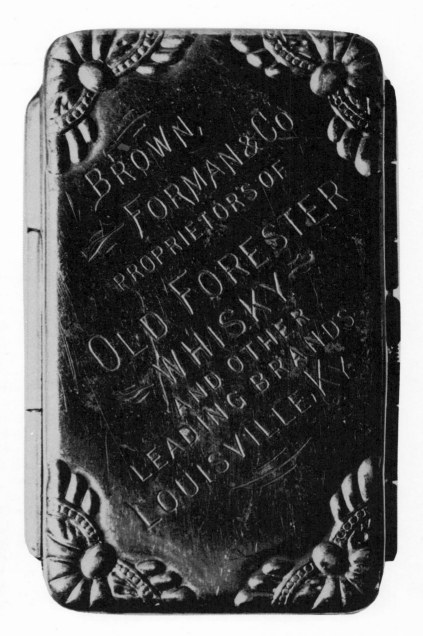

SILVER PLATED MATCH SAFE
Before the days of pocket lighters, these were highly-prized premiums. This match case was distributed by Brown-Forman in the early 1900's.

1907 HEINZ DEMITASSE SPOON
From 1907 to 1932, these silver plated demitasse spoons were given as mementos to visitors touring the Heinz plant in Pittsburgh. In the bowl of the spoon, in relief, is a picture of the Pittsburgh office and factory.

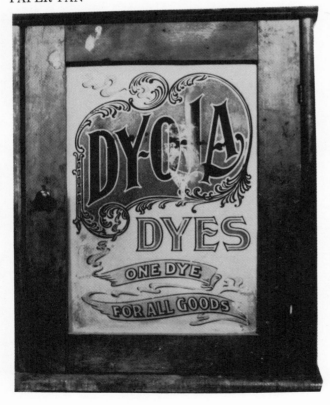

PAPER FAN

COURTESY HARRIET REBARBER

WOOD CABINET

H. J. HEINZ COMPANY

The year 1869 produced more than its share of turning points in world history. Seeking to restore unity after a bloody civil war, the United States installed a hero of that day, Ulysses S. Grant, as its 18th President. The Vatican convened its first General Council in three centuries. The Suez Canal was officially opened, altering the patterns of trade and empire. In the light of those monumental events, historians of the time were not likely to note what must have seemed a minor development, the founding of H. J. Heinz Company in 1869.

Some years before, young Henry J. Heinz had tended a vegetable garden outside his family's home at Sharpsburg, Pennsylvania. His sense of seed and soil led to a surplus, which he sold to his neighbors. By the time he was 16, he had progressed from basket to wheelbarrow to horse drawn wagon, and was selling to grocers in Pittsburgh, five miles downriver.

Heinz' first processed product was horse-radish, a preparation of great popularity in that area at the time, but one acquired mainly at the cost of scraped knuckles and housewife's tears. Henry Heinz packed his horse-radish in bottles of clear glass to show that he had used no turnip filler.

He has been described as an early genius in advertising and marketing. He hit on the magic "57" with a sure feel for the effect of that number. The slogan came to be recognized on every continent. Heinz ordered the erection of New York's first electric sign, a six-story, 1,200-light display that advertised "good things for the table" from Heinz.

He transformed Heinz from a local into a national company with the opening of a Philadelphia sales branch in 1882, and into an international marketer in 1886, when he personally secured an order for the entire Heinz line from Britain's venerable Fortnum and Mason. In 1905, H. J. Heinz Company, Ltd., the first overseas operation, was born with the acquisition of a small factory in London.

Early in the 20th century the founder and his son, Howard Heinz, threw their considerable prestige behind the campaign that led to the passage of the Pure Food Law in 1906. Unlike many of their contemporaries, they realized the need to build confidence among consumers who still tended to suspect any foods not prepared in their own kitchens.

Heinz-in-1969 had 17 companies around the world, operating 40 plants in 13 nations and territories. It made more than 1,250 products, which were marketed in more than 150 nations.

SHOWCASES

During the late 19th century and well into the present one, merchants bought a great variety of bulk products. Therefore, showcases in many different sizes and shapes filled every available space in the country store, from the oiled wood floor, to the embossed tin ceiling. Some were elegantly constructed, with the company name lithographed, stenciled, or etched into the beveled glass windows. And occasionally a company name would be applied by a decal.

Showcases were not only a means of preserving a product, but provided a means of pushing the name of a product and the company name to prominence.

Today decorators as well as collectors find many uses for old showcases, regardless of size or shape. Many are especially useful for storing small collections of toys, dolls, bottles, etc., depending upon one's ingenuity.

STATIONERY ITEMS

The tools and supplies used to conduct business make up another field of potential advertising collectibles. These items include letter openers, pencil cases, calendars, erasers, blotters, book marks, rulers, measuring tapes, pencils, pen racks, string holders, inkwells, and all other paraphernalia used in offices.

TRINKETS

Trinkets were also given by commercial firms for promotional purposes. This group of collectibles includes various charms, such as a miniature Swift's Premium Ham, or a little green pickle which promoted Heinz pickles. Whistles, the cricket noise maker, badges, and advertising pins and buttons are also very popular today.

GLASS PROJECTION SLIDES

There is a growing interest today in the early colored, double glass projection slides that were used by movie houses to advertise products or coming attractions during the silent film days. The value of material in this field of advertising is influenced strongly by the product or by the star involved in the coming attraction.

TOY BUS

BISCUIT CUTTER: MEASURING SPOONS: STRAINERS

NOVELTY CLOCK

123

1909 ADVERTISING SHEET MUSIC

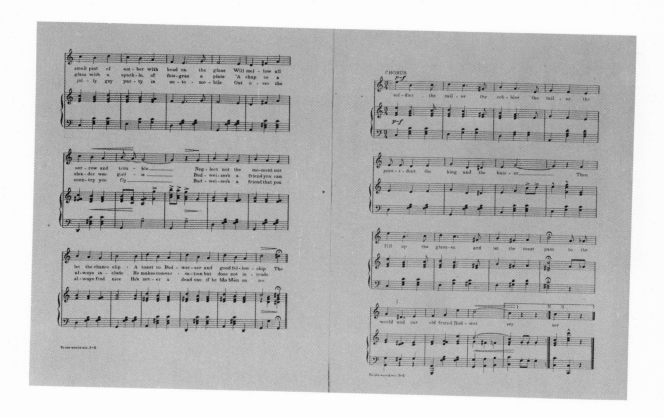

ADVERTISING SHEET MUSIC

It will surprise many advertising enthusiasts to learn that sheet music is related to advertising through various early compositions that were published by or for business firms and products. The attractive and interesting illustrations on the fronts of these mementos fit very well with any collection of advertising material. Early examples date in the 1850-1880 period, while later ones were published during the early years or the present century. Some of the titles include:

ANILINE POLKA MAZURKA, 1869 (Aniline Dye & Chemical).

GOOD OLD SWEET HAM, 1873 (Magnolia Hams).

HAVE YOU A LITTLE FAIRY IN YOUR HOME? 1920-30 (Fairy Soap).

MY COCA-COLA GIRL, 1920-30.

NUMBER 3, 1920-30 (Old Gold Cigarettes).

SMOKE YOUR TROUBLES AWAY, 1920-30 (Henry George Cigars).

STANDARD OIL, 1907.

THE BLACK COOK, 1867 (Charter Oak Ranges).

THE MAKIN'S OF THE U.S.A. (Bull Durham).

THE MOXIE ONE STEP, 1920-30.

TO THE WORLD AND BUDWEISER.

RARE CIGAR TIN
Made in the shape of a stein, rare tin has colorful, embossed decoration. Printed on base: "Factory No. 153, Dist. State of Nebr." 5½" high, 3¾" diameter.

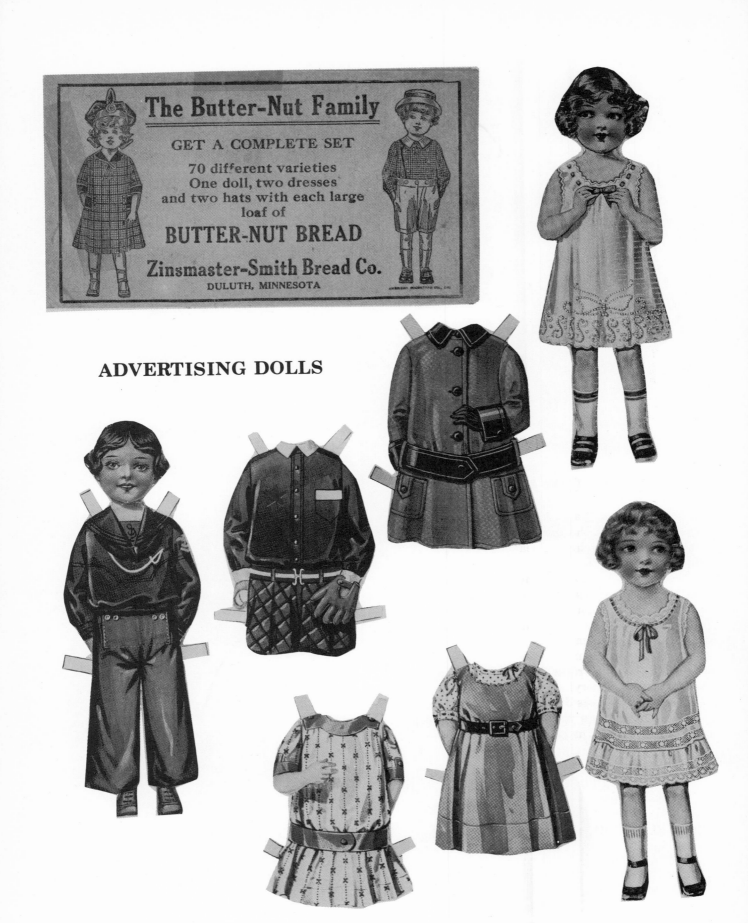

The Butter-Nut Family

GET A COMPLETE SET

70 different varieties
One doll, two dresses
and two hats with each large
loaf of

BUTTER-NUT BREAD

Zinsmaster-Smith Bread Co.
DULUTH, MINNESOTA

ADVERTISING DOLLS

WATCH FOBS; KEY CHAINS; STICK PIN; BOTTLE OPENER

ADVERTISING WATCH FOBS

The advertising watch fobs appeared in considerable number about the turn of the present century. Their popularity reached its peak shortly after World War I.

Early fobs were made of metals and other materials, with pictures appearing on the front of many and advertising on the back. Those issued by the John Deere Company used pearl in which to mount the company's emblem.

Men in particular like to collect watch fobs, specializing in types representing automobiles, railroads, farm machinery, steam engines, fire engines, road equipment, presidential and commemorative themes. Other types were issued by companies to promote such things as coffee, beverages, shoes, etc.

COURTESY DOROTHY VANIS

MOTTLED POTTERY PITCHER

127